The Mark Degree

The Mark Degree

David Mitchell

'A truly fascinating book, perfect for all Freemasons'

The privacy of the Mark Degree in this book is well protected. *The Mark Degree* should be an essential part of the reading of every mason, members of the Craft as well as Mark Masons, an integral part of Freemasonry, both Operative and Speculative. Approved as such in 1856 by the then Pro Grand Master, the Earl of Zetland, the Mark Degree was nevertheless rejected by United Grand Lodge. Here is the veritable story of a rejected 'Stone' which possessed merits and qualities then unknown, and which ultimately became the Headstone of an esteemed and distinguished structure.

WBro David Mitchell PAGDC, PPrGJW (London),
PPrGReg (Gloucestershire and Herefordshire), PRAMGR
Author,
June 2002

Lewis Masonic

First published 2003

ISBN 0 85318 2299

Published by Lewis Masonic

an imprint of Ian Allan Publishing Ltd,
Hersham, Surrey KT12 4RG.
Printed by Ian Allan Printing Ltd,
Hersham, Surrey KT12 4RG.

Contents

Foreword

WBro David Mitchell, a Mark Mason for some thirty-five years, writes with a skilful pen to produce a guided and in-depth appraisal of the Master's duties and the responsibilities for his Officers. This is related against the background of Mark Masonry, and 'Chusing the Mark', from the time of the building of King Solomon's Temple to the formation of Mark Grand Lodge.

Interesting, informative and instructive, the book should prove of great value to all Mark Masons and provide the new Advancee with a wealth of knowledge to prepare him for every office on his way to the Master's Chair.

This is a book which will prove of equal interest to members of the Craft who are not Mark Masons.

T J Lewis
Grand Secretary
Grand Lodge of Mark Master Masons
June 2002

Introduction

Over the years, Freemasonry is fortunate in having been well supplied with excellent books of research and instruction, by many learned and sincere Masons. In the Mark Masons' Degree, however, it would seem that there is room for a book other than just an instruction manual, to be addressed to Masters of Lodges, Masters-elect and Officers as well as of benefit to Advancees, explaining the ideals of this lovely Degree and helping its readers to reach ever-higher standards of understanding and perfection in its ceremonial.

The book, titled simply *The Mark Degree*, fills this gap neatly. I believe it should be a 'must' in every Mark Master Mason's bookcase. Its author WBro David Mitchell shows a firm grasp of Lodge procedure. This work will surely prove of immense value to all its readers. Written with much skill, certain features which are confidential to Mark Masonry are carefully preserved, making the book a fascinating and compelling read for members of the Craft as well as Mark Masons.

It is expected that this book will increase the interest and expertise of *all Freemasons*, and not only those in the Mark Degree, with its symbolism and message of a task well performed.

The later chapters contain a wealth of little-known information and bring together the correct procedures and true understanding of the ritual as well as of the history of Masonic craftsmen from the mists of the past.

A truly fascinating book, perfect for all Freemasons.

VWBro B Macdean Ross, PGJO, ProvGSW (London)
Editor
June 2002

Acknowledgements

This book is dedicated to my wife Eileen without whose patience, tolerance and understanding it could never have been written.

Anyone who writes on the subject of Freemasonry is soon to realise that there is one great fount of knowledge he cannot ignore. 'Transactions of Ars Quatuor Coronatorum'. (Transactions of Quatuor Coronati Lodge No. 2076, familiarly known as AQC). I am very grateful to AQC, for the many authoritative articles written on the subject of Mark Masonry and on Masonry in general. Also to several other literary sources of information to which I shall give mention in a short bibliography of recommended reading.

In the compilation of this book I have read literally thousands of pages of books and articles relevant to the subject matter and in many instances I have been able to acknowledge the source in the text. However, I wish to make special mention of the late Worshipful Brother Major Clement Whitlock Cowell affectionately known as 'Daddy'. Daddy Cowell was a Founder and first Secretary of my Mother Lodge of Mark Master Masons, the King Solomon's Quarries Lodge MMM No. 828 Jerusalem, now meeting at Mark Masons' Hall, St. James, London. A lot of Daddy Cowell's knowledge of the history and geography of Jerusalem is reflected in this book, knowledge which gained him the reputation as 'The father of English Masonry in the Holy Land'. I am also indebted to 'Daddy' for the rare and interesting photographs illustrated in this book.

My grateful thanks also to several Grand Officers who made time to read the manuscript of this book and for their encouragement and suggestions, especially during the period when their time and energies were heavily committed to the success of the Festival of the Anniversary of the Grand Lodge of Mark Master Masons' Fund of Benevolence. They are Right Worshipful Brother David Ivor Williams, Provincial Grand Master for London. VWBro Brian Anthony Vickers, PGMO and Deputy Provincial Grand Master for London.

RWBro Desmond Bowditch, GJW, and MBF Administrator.

WBro Nigel Franklin, BA (Hons), PGStdB, for his professionalism in preparation of the final pages for the printer.

And finally my Editor VWBro B Macdean Ross, PGJO for his tremendous support and encouragement as well as his professional expertise in communications.

Author's Preface

Many learned and influential Freemasons believed earnestly that 'Chusing his mark' was in addition to being an important part of the Fellowcrafts' Degree, an integral part of the qualifications for the Degree of Mark Master Mason. Our Masonic Grandfathers in United Grand Lodge rejected such a proposal. However, today, some 150 years later, Mark Masonry is a separate Degree and thrives under the aegis of its own Grand Lodge of Mark Master Masons. Bernard E Jones, in his excellent book, *Freemasons' Guide and Compendium*, writes, 'One of the soundest of our Masonic Writers has said that the Mark Degree, although not recognised as part of the Craft system of Freemasonry, *should be supported and practised for its antiquity as well as for the beauty and teaching of its ritual.*'

Today, Mark Masons are proud to be known as belonging to 'The Friendly Degree'. In the bar at Mark Masons' Hall, St James, in London, I overheard a comment, *'In all my years as a Mark Mason I have never met anyone who did not thoroughly enjoy belonging to this degree.'* I would endorse this statement and add that in my thirty-five years a Mark Mason I have enjoyed the meetings and the friendship of Brethren in London, the Home Counties, and other Provinces throughout England and Wales. We are indeed 'The Friendly Degree', which has put a special emphasis on Brotherly Love and placed upon our Brother the highest possible valuation as a friend and companion.

It is also true to say, notwithstanding this, that over the years we have failed to give to the practice of our Ritual the full and dedicated attention it deserves. Today our ceremonies in Lodges are better than they were some fifteen years ago. Then, it was not uncommon for the Master and his Officers to work the Ceremony from the little books. Also the demonstration of the Signs was much varied. One sad result was that the sign m was seldom given and nearly became extinct. Very few Mark Masons knew the Word well enough to pronounce it properly. Fortunately those days are in the past, but there are still too many occasions when the small books are used in Lodge through lack of preparation. There is, of course, no substitute for a good Lodge of Instruction. Regrettably in Mark Masonry these are few and far between. Even if we had them we have to face the fact that our Mark Brother is also a member of the Craft where the traditional procedures and disciplines are somewhat stricter. He may likewise be a Royal Arch Mason. And there are yet additional Masonic interests. A Freemason today is more than likely to have responsibility in business with consequent commitments and pressures. A good Mason should also give as a priority an ample portion of his time to his wife and family, contingency time involvement, personal physical constraint and time to relax.

WHAT THEN IS THE ANSWER?

A practical solution to this difficult question may be found in a book specially written to deal with the problem. Countless voluminous tomes have been written on the subject of Freemasonry during the last three centuries. Many are abstruse and embarrassingly difficult to understand. I do not wish to add to the heap but we do seem to lack in Mark Masonry a concise, simple, almost elementary book which can be readily understood and absorbed at one reading. A book which, read as a supplement to the ritual, would indicate to the Brother not only *what* to do but *how* to do it. It has been said that the Mark Degree lends itself to a certain freedom of expression. Specially attractive perhaps to the budding actor. Let us develop this. Such a book would contain the stage scenery in the form of a historical background to the Degree.

The Mark Degree does this in a simple, easy to understand way. It does more! It relates in the same simple style brief details of the materials for the Temple. For example, 'Stone', the instrument of the Mark Master's craft. The Cedars of Lebanon, the responsibility of Adoniram. The Clay Ground in the plain of Jordan between Succoth and Zeredatha producing the best obtainable clay for the casting of moulds. A colourful background to enhance the narrative of the 'incident' and inspire the 'persons represented' with the reserve power to feel involved and each to communicate his role with spirit and feeling rather than just recite to each other memorised words.

Next is included an appraisal of the desirable pursuit of each officer in the Lodge and suggested areas for improvement. This may sound a little presumptuous and arrogant but observations over the years have thrown up a pattern of behaviour. And as members of the Lodge tend to follow in the footsteps of those who preceded them, the pattern is hard to break. Nothing of course that regular attendance at a good Lodge of Instruction could not handle competently. But this is not the prevailing system of things. It is, however, an opportunity to *see oursels as others see us* to quote Robert Burns. The 'Written Rehearsal' is concerned with the Opening and Closing of the Lodge. And the Ceremony of Advancement. If you like, what can and does happen 'on the night'. Strengths as well as areas of weakness are highlighted and appropriate suggestions are made.

A Ceremony which makes a lasting impression on the Candidate and enriches his enjoyment of the Mark Degree is also a Ceremony which must give satisfaction and a sense of achievement to the officers involved.

The Mark Degree is a book to be given to a Candidate on the night of his advancement into Mark Masonry. He will find it a valuable source of reference as he progresses through the various offices to the Master's Chair. It therefore follows that each and every Mark Mason will find it equally beneficial, Past Masters and all. It should be referred to before each meeting and read conjointly with the revision of the ritual.

If *The Mark Degree* has any advantage at all over a Lodge of Instruction, it is that it need never be more than a few steps away from your favourite armchair.

Good luck and Mark well!

Bibliography

Here are a number of books and other sources of information which the Author found helpful in his researches. The reader may also find them interesting and helpful for reference and general background information.

Up-to-date Mark Ritual. To include lecture on the Mark Master Masons' Degree and Lecture on the Tracing Board;

Transactions of Quatuor Coronati Lodge No. 2076;

Holy Bible. Masonic Edition;

The Jerusalem Bible, Darton, Longman and Todd, London;

The Oxford Companion to the Bible, Oxford University Press;

The Bible as History Revised by Werner Keller, Book Club Associates;

Josephus, Complete Works. Includes the Antiquities of the Jews and The Wars of the Jews. Pickering and Inglis Ltd, London;

King Solomon's Temple in the Masonic Tradition by Alex Horne, The Aquarian Press. Wellingborough, Northamptonshire;

The Encyclopedia of the Bible, Lion Publishing;

Langenscheidt's 'The Experienced Traveler's Guide to Israel', Langenscheidt Publishers Inc, Maspeth New York 11378;

The Israelites by B S J Isserlin, Thames and Hudson, Bloomsbury Street, London WC1B 3QP;

Encyclopaedia Britannica, Encyclopaedia Britannica Limited, London;

And highly recommended to all Freemasons, the 'Freemasons' Guide and Compendium' by Bernard E Jones, George E Harrap and Company, London.

Mark Masonry

Origins and Early Development

Over the years there has been much speculation concerning the source of Masonry by many interested and well-intentioned Freemasons. As a result Masonry has from time to time been discredited by conflicting and at times extravagant and reckless claims by seemingly authoritative writers.

Since there is no known authentic account of the origin of most Masonic Degrees, most writers have, in good faith, established their 'facts' from ancient lore and the story of the building of King Solomon's Temple. The History of the Mark Degree is no exception and has like the other Degrees been very much dependent on the writings of the Holy Bible and on classic works such as those of Flavius Josephus the Jewish historian.

However, in the 18th and 19th centuries there are several instances of erudite and respected Masons making unequivocal statements which would appear to go beyond the limits of credibility. For example, William Preston, (1742–1818), after whom the esteemed Prestonian Lectures are named, once wrote, *'From the commencement of the World we may trace the foundations of Freemasonry.'* The Reverend George Oliver (1782–1867) stated, *'Ancient Masonic Traditions say, and I think justly so, that our Ancient Science existed before the Creation of this Globe, and was diffused amidst the various systems of Space.'*

All things are possible and the beliefs of such two celebrated and scholarly Masons, whose prolific writings on Masonry are today still widely read and quoted, may be true; but there is no known proof. A more modern and conservative writer Robert Freke Gould, whose many writings include the monumental *The History of Freemasonry*, written in three volumes between 1882 and 1887, was much more sceptical. He would accept nothing without evidence and confirmation of facts. There is no reason why we should not enjoy the ingenuity and fertility of some of those early writers but like Robert Gould accept nothing as true without evidence.

The beginning of Mark Masonry is somewhat obscure. Before we become entangled in its legendary Traditional History and its earlier development, it will be useful if we have a close look at some hard facts concerning Freemasonry in general. The only documentary evidence we possess of an antiquity of more than some three and a half centuries is:

– Certain references in the 14th century to the 'Gild of Masons', the London Company, and individual Freemasons;

– Reference in the Statutes beginning in 1349 in the reign of Edward III and going down to the reign of Elizabeth I, (1558–1603).

– A series of documents known as the 'Old Charges' dating from the 16th century. These attestations written for and by rulers of the Craft contain a legendary history as well as rules for the guidance of the Craft and of the individual Masters, Fellowcrafts and Apprentices;

– Two manuscripts, (extant), older than any known version of the 'Old Charges'. They are the *Regius Poem* known as the *Halliwell Manuscript* dated about 1389, and the *Cooke Manuscript* dated some thirty or forty years later. Both the Regius and Cooke manuscripts can be seen in the British Museum;

– *The Schaw Statutes* or ordinances of 1598 and 1599 which specify four Scottish Lodges then in existence. These Statutes also contain the rules and regulations for the government of the Craft;

– Minutes of the meetings of Scottish Lodges going back to the year 1599. There appear to be no minutes of English Lodges before the year 1700;

– Literature of the 17th century containing numerous Masonic references by antiquaries and other sources.

Some of our scholarly Brethren in the past, always in good faith I'm sure, have been much too ready to jump to hasty conclusions and see similarities of Masonic ritual in a Druidical Initiation Ceremony. They have compared some of our Signs with those of Australian aborigines or regarded ancient carvings of our working tools in a catacomb or certain signs carved in stone discovered in Baalbek or Capernaum as evidence which proves or even tends to prove a Masonic existence in early history.

See photograph page 15, Masons will readily recognise the objects in this photograph as Working Tools. They are funeral emblems buried with Sennuten of Thebes in the 20th Dynasty, that is 1200 to 1090BC. They can be viewed in Room 17, Case 2015 at the Egyptian Museum in Cairo. Nevertheless, perhaps regrettably, we cannot without adequate proof claim our origins or ritual from the time of the building of the Pyramids, even though Mark Masons will have an inkling of some of the skills and intricate procedures involved in the construction of such a prodigious project.

Funeral Emblems
Buried with Sennuten of
Thebes, 20th Dynasty —
1200–1090BC.
Can be viewed in Case 2015,
Room 17, Egyptian Museum,
Cairo.

In this frame of mind we may allow ourselves to be guided safely into the exegesis of the Mark Masons lectures and ritual. And at this stage it is right and proper to emphasise that the Mark Master Mason is already a Master Craftsman and subject to all his former obligations. The three Great Lights are still the same three Great Lights. The obligations and teachings are of course supplementary and additional to those of the former degrees.

The lecture on the Mark Master Masons' Degree begins:

'At the building of King Solomon's Temple and before the institution of the degree of Master Mason and Past Master, there were 80,000 operatives employed, part of

whom were hewers in the quarries at Zaradatha, and part builders of the Temple; besides these there was a levy of 30,000 in the forests of Lebanon. In order that each of the 110,000 workmen might be known to his superior officers, every portion of the work be subject to the nicest scrutiny, and each Fellow Craft receive with punctuality the reward of his industry and skill, this immense number was divided into 1100 Lodges of Fellow Crafts and Entered Apprentices, the latter under the superintendence of the former who taught them the work; and over the whole presided 3000 Menatschin, Overseers or Masters, three over each Lodge.'

The project of the building of King Solomon's Temple could hardly have been feasible without some functional organisation to ensure that each of the 110,000 workmen received his wages. And, of course, that no one received his wages more than once. Also to ensure that each workman received no more than his due: Mark Men nine shekels a day, and Mark Masters 25 shekels a day. We already know the means by which the Fellow Craftsmen were prevented from receiving the wages of the Mark Masters. The Mark Men or Fellow Craftsmen were most certainly recognised as undisputed experts of their craft. The Mark Masters however were on a higher plane and known to be *Perfect* Craftsmen. It was from such Mark Masters that the Overseers were selected. Adoniram who was an Overseer was selected to fill the vacancy occasioned by the death of Hiram Abif. Adoniram was in fact the Chief Overseer of the levy employed in the forests of Lebanon which numbered 30,000 men. He sent them to the forests in monthly relays of 10,000, so that the men spent one month in the Lebanon and two months at home. See 1 Kings, chapter 5, Vs 13 and 14. They received their wages at their place of work.

The Craftsmen and others, of course, received their wages at the Temple: the Apprentices in corn, wine and oil; the Craftsmen in hard coin. The ritual tells us that they went to the middle *Chamber* of the Temple to be paid. The word *Chamber* cannot be correct. In all probability it is a wrong translation of the word for Court or Courtyard. If we examine Schick's Model of King Solomon's Temple and the Temple area,opposite, this will give us some idea how the Temple and its surrounds may have looked. As you will see there is no shortage of courtyards or 'court' type areas next to buildings. One has to concede that climbing a spiral staircase would be feasible. What is extremely difficult to imagine is how hundreds of men could have assembled in a single chamber described as being seven cubits long by seven cubits wide. The length of a cubit was estimated to measure between eighteen and twenty-one inches. If we settle for twenty-one inches then we are talking about a room a fraction larger than four yards by four yards, the approximate dimensions of a modern medium size bedroom. Now if the Temple took seven years to build we are more likely to be talking about the earlier stages of its construction rather than the completion. In which case this 'Chamber' is more than likely to have been only partially completed, if even that, but leaving us with plenty of courtyards conveniently sited.

The important factor, however, is that the craftsmen and others did receive their wages. And so the building of the Temple advanced.

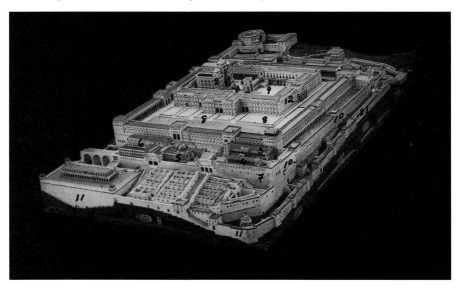

Schick's Model of King Solomon's Temple and the Temple Site

1	Tower of Hananeel	7	King Solomon's Stables
2	The Temple	8	Outer Court of the Israelites
3	King Solomon's Palace	9	Court of the Sanhedrin
4	Queen's Palace	10	Temple Wall
5	Court of Justice	11	City Wall
6	House of Cedars of Lebanon	12	The Gate Beautiful

To ensure progress and the smooth running and efficiency of many diverse operations there had to be strict organisational procedures and progress systems for stones to be hewn, inspected and passed, then eventually fitted in their proper places.

This is where the *Mason's Mark* played an all important role. Each workman had his own mark which would be carved or indented on a blocked-out stone. The Overseer, who was familiar with the marks of the members of his team, a group of men who would work, eat and lodge together, was able to examine the work submitted to him and compare it with his plans. If the stone was correct and in accordance with his plans, the Overseer fixed his own mark upon it, at the same time reconciling it with his marks on previous stones examined and passed. Each stone would then be rolled down the slope and compared with corresponding plans on the site. Once finally approved by the Master Overseer and indented with the triangle, it was hauled up and set in its correct place. More than likely an Overseer's mark would indicate the exact location of the stone when a wooden maul was all that was needed to align the stone firmly and permanently in its proper position.

Masons' Marks were thus a vital aid to the management functions of administration, finance, production and quality control. The Mason's Mark was the visible sign or identity mark of the individual craftsman who used it as a signature. It attested that the completed work on which the mark had been made was solely his own work and that he alone had earned the wages due. In the event of faulty work it enabled the Overseer to identify the craftsman responsible. The finished stones once approved were, as earlier described, deposited in their proper places in accordance with the site plan with greater facility and precision. Building progress and efficiency was dependent in those days, as it is now, on good communications to and fro, good relations between and among the workmen, respect for management and enthusiasm and enjoyment on the job. All these qualities were in turn dependent on the *Mason's Mark.*

The Graham Manuscript of 1726 was discovered in Ireland only sixty-six years ago in 1936. It contains a passage on the payment of the workmen of much interest to Mark Master Masons:

'Now it is holden fforth by tradition that there was a tumult at this erection, (*The Temple*), which should (*not have*) hapened betwext the labourers and masons about wages; and ffor to calm all and make things easie, the wise King should have said Be all of you contented ffor you shall be payed all alike; yet give a signe to the masons not known to the labourers, (*who were not Masons*), and whoever could make that signe at the paying-place was to be payed as masons, the labourers not knowing thereof were payed as aforesaid'.

Bearing in mind that the *Graham Manuscript* of 1726 is among the earliest extant documents known to us on Mark Masonry, we readily recognise the 'incident' as being akin to our modern-day ritual.

A number of Masonic writers have attempted to associate Masons' Marks with magical and esoteric practices such as Cabbala, (oral tradition of the Jews said to have been handed down from Moses), and other doctrines which flourished in ancient Egypt. Today Masons' Marks are regarded by serious students and writers of Masonic material as being of a strictly practical nature, fundamentally to identify the man who shaped the stone, and to indicate where and in what position the stone should be laid. The placing of a mark on a finished product was not a practice exclusive to stone masons. Early history tells us of ancient fabrics from Eastern countries bearing the weaver's mark. Ancient pottery relating to the Roman occupation of Britain is still being found bearing such marks. Mediaeval goldsmiths and silversmiths made their exclusive marks on their valuable creations and ware to indicate the quality of the article as well as to identify the craftsman. Cutters and joiners had their individual marks. In France we are told by Levasseur, a celebrated authority, that Goldsmiths, Clothworkers, Potters, Coopers and nearly every class of artisan possessed their stamp or private mark. The assessors were the recipients and depositaries for the safe keeping of the common seal of the craft and they placed it on all articles inspected and approved by them. (*Histoires des Classes Ouvrières en France*).

In Scotland bakers as well as masons made their marks on their produce. In 1398 magistrates in Aberdeen ordered every baker to mark his loaves so that a sample of contaminated or adulterated bread could be traced to its origin and maker. Indeed such marks are believed to be still very much in existence, generally in the form of a circle comprising a varying number of dots.

A much more exciting and compelling question must be — 'Was the stone mason the *first* craftsman to mark or indent his finished product?' The operative Mason's Mark has been found on the stonework of buildings of the Egyptians, Assyrians, Babylonians and Greeks, and upon stones used in building by almost every nation in the ancient world.

In Ireland, Scotland, England and Wales, masons' Marks are to be found on stones in Cathedrals, Churches, Castles and other mediaeval buildings. In 1949, workmen installing a new ventilation unit for the House of Commons disclosed some pieces of history which had been hidden since the 11th century: chisel marks and signs put on the stones by the masons building the Cloisters at the Chapel of Saint Stephen.

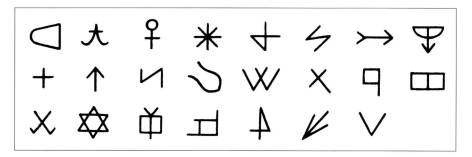

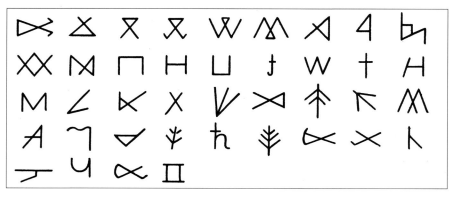

Masons' Marks
A sample of some historic Masons' Marks found in the Tower at Chester.
Marks in the first row appear in the crypt. The second row are marks found on the risers to the steps to the chapel; and the final row from the ancient chapel itself. (Top)
More Masons' Marks from the Church at Holt, near Wrexham. (Above)

The earliest stone masons must have wished to build some form of shelter to protect their families from marauders as well as the elements. Nor can we deny them the need for self expression, to create things and feel subsequent pride in the finished product, a creative urge or instinct perhaps to shape the form of their gods. And why should they not wish to build a place to worship these gods? And of course they had a pride in the skill of their workmanship, and the means to improve those skills without which there could hardly have been progress. And from that inevitably came the desire to identify their work by means of a Sign or Mark, gratifying dominant human needs which we call today Pride, Job Satisfaction and a Sense of Importance. The stone mason may therefore have been the first artisan to mark his work. But we cannot know for certain, there is no known proof. As suggested earlier we should accept nothing without conclusive evidence. Who knows? There are still many desert caves in Israel, Palestine and surrounding lands which might in the future produce great antiquities for Freemasonry in general. Our own 'Dead Sea Scrolls' so to speak.

We go to Scotland to find our earliest surviving records of Brethren recording their 'Marks' in Lodge. The earliest Lodge Minutes (extant), dated 31st July, 1599 of St Mary's Chapel Lodge of Edinburgh is confirmed by the Mark of the Warden. The old Mark Book of 1670 belonging to the Lodge of Aberdeen No. 1 ter is probably the oldest surviving record of Brethren recording their Marks in a Lodge, the book being described as 'having a beautiful record of Marks dating back to 1670'. Still, there is no record or other evidence of any ceremony being held or ritual worked. At this stage we must of necessity allow ourselves a little licence, notwithstanding our resolve to accept nothing without proof.

Being made a Mark Man or a Mark Master would be no mean achievement and it must therefore have been a very special occasion for a Mason. An award on such a special occasion would involve some sort of formal presentation or 'ceremony', however slight. Following such a presentation, it is not too difficult to imagine the new Mark Mason inviting his friends along for a drink and something to eat. A small private room in the hostelry perhaps where the landlord's wife would serve them a meal.

Such happenings are implied in the following extracts taken from the important and much quoted Schaw Statutes (1598) mentioned earlier. The Schaw Statutes were rules, regulations and ordinances laid down for Scottish Operative Masons by William Schaw, Chief Master Mason to the King of Scotland, King James VI:

'No Master or Fellowcraft may be received or admitted except in the presence of six Masters and two Entered Apprentices, the Warden of that Lodge being one of the six, the date thereof being orderly booked and his 'Name and Mark' insert in the said book, together with the names of the six Masters, the Apprentices, and the Intender, (presumably the Proposer). No one is to be admitted without an assay and trial of skill.'

Yet another extract from the second set of Schaw Statutes reads:

'…Fellowcrafts at entry and prior to admission must pay to the Lodge ten pounds and ten shillings worth of Gloves*, this including the expense of the Banquet, and none are to be admitted without 'One sufficient assay and proof of memory and craft'.'

* 'Gloves' meant Glove money, in other words a perquisite or a little something for yourself. It was also frequently used as a name for a bribe.

Brother Doctor G C Coulton records in his book, *Art and the Reformation* '…but we do hear of the Ceremonial adoption of the 'Mark' in Germany. The first definite and explicit evidence apparently comes from the *Torgau Statutes of 1462*. 'The journeyman took his Mark at a solemn admission-feast. Partly at the Master's expense and partly at his own. In Lodge he was forbidden to engrave his work until the stone had been inspected and passed by the Master of the Lodge or the Warden.'

From these example records of operative masons in Scotland and on the continent of Europe, we can readily detect the ceremonial inference of the very special occasion of *'Chusing the Mark'*, and of course the 'Banquet' which followed. These events would later be given even greater prominence or distinction in the future Ceremonies worked by the Speculative Masons.

Moving on from Operative Masonry to Speculative Masonry, the earliest record yet discovered in Scotland of the 'Mark' being worked in a Lodge as a Masonic Degree is to be found in the minutes of the Lodge St John Operative at Banff, 7th July, 1788. There is also circumstantial evidence of the Mark Degree being worked some eighteen years earlier in Dumfries in 1770. This earliest record of the Mark in connection with Speculative Masonry refers to the *Royal Arch Degree*. The Journeyman Lodge of Dumfries, now the Thistle Lodge No. 62, records on the 8th October 1770, the elevation of a Brother to the Degree of Royal Arch Mason and in the course of a form of certificate, lists his qualifications as Entered Apprentice, Fellowcraft, Master, Mark Master Mason, Master of the Chair, Sublime Degree of Excellent, and Super-Excellent Royal Arch Mason.

In England the earliest record of Mark Masonry in a Speculative body is dated 1st September 1769. It is contained in the opening minutes of the Royal Arch Chapter of Friendship, now No. 257 of Portsmouth. It is written in Cypher and is translated thus…'At a Royal Arch Chapter held at the George Tavern, Portsmouth, on the 1st September 1769. Present Thomas Dunckerley Esq William Cook 'Z'. Samual Palmer 'H'. Thomas Scanville as 'J'. Henry Dean, Phillip Joyes and Thomas Webb. The Provincial Grand Master Thomas Dunckerley brought the Warrant of the Chapter, and having lately received the 'Mark' he made the Brethren *Mark Masons* and *Mark Masters*, and each chuse their Mark.'

The importance of these minutes cannot be overemphasised, stated or measured since Thomas Dunckerley refers to the *Mark Degree* as a going concern. The two degrees were conferred much as they are today, the Fellowcraft eligible to become a *Mark Man* and the Master Mason a *Mark Master*. English Masonry now more or less combines them but elsewhere they are still worked as separate degrees. The next reference to the *Mark Degree* in England in point of time is found in the Minute Book of the Marquis of Granby Lodge No. 124 Durham, and is dated 21st December, 1773. This entry states that 'Brother Barwick was also made a Mark Mason and Brother James McKinley was raised to the sublime Degree of Master Mason, and also made a *Mark Mason* and paid accordingly.'

The Minute Books of the Craft Lodge of Friendship No. 277, Oldham in Lancashire contains records of the making of Mark Masons from 1795 to 1838.

On the consolidation of English Craft Masonry by the Union of the two Grand Lodges on December 27th 1813, twenty-one Articles of Union were drawn up and signed by the two Grand Masters, The Duke of Sussex and Edward, Duke of Kent.

Article No. 2 provided: 'It is declared and pronounced that pure ancient Masonry consists of *Three Degrees* and no more; viz. those of Entered Apprentice, Fellowcraft, and Master Mason including the Supreme Order of the Holy Royal Arch. But this Article is not intended to prevent any Lodge or Chapter from holding a Meeting in any of the Degrees of the Orders of Chivalry according to the Constitutions of the said Orders.'

The effect of this Declaration of 'Three Degrees and no more' on the Additional Degrees, many of which were working under Craft Warrants, was disastrous. A goodly number of the degrees affected were defiant and tried to continue but were subdued and eventually disintegrated under the severe, indeed harsh regime of the Duke of Sussex who had a reputation of being an autocrat. On the other hand, a number of Mark Lodges persisted in spite of Article 2 of the Union. In Scotland and Ireland the position differed entirely from England since the Mark Degree was an essential qualification for the Royal Arch.

In England, although the position of Mark Masonry was somewhat chaotic and Masons resentful and rebellious, the Degree continued to be conferred under the Banner of Craft Lodges and in addition under such quaint Masonic fellowships as *Travelling Lodges*. For example, there was the famous Travelling Lodge of Ashton-under-Lyne. The Lodge met on a Sunday, loaded up its Masonic paraphernalia on to a horse and cart and set off for the meeting place of the Craft Lodge under whose Banner it was to meet, be it Cheshire, Lancashire or Yorkshire. The local Host Lodge would open up to the third Degree. The Mark Brethren then entered, took over the Chairs before opening in the Mark Degree and advancing such Brethren as presented themselves. The ritual which the Travelling Mark Lodge worked differed somewhat from the ritual to which we are accustomed. One particular was to lift a peculiarly shaped stone in a particular manner. The Candidate would be called upon to receive a Brother's Mark in accordance with his Obligation. He would be given instruction in the 'secret alphabet of a mark master mason' which we would recognise as the Masonic Cypher.

In Scotland, the Grand Lodge of Scotland officially abandoned the Mark Degree in 1800, when the first of the Acts against Secret Societies became Law in 1799. The Grand Lodge of Scotland, however, did not appear to have been too strict on 'Daughter Lodges' as to which Degrees were to be worked. It was only when it suddenly and without warning found itself in the invidious position of certifying to the Officers of the Crown for the behaviour of those Lodges, 'within the meaning of the Act', that it realised that it could only functionally do so by prohibiting all Lodges from working any Degrees other than Entered Apprentice, Fellowcraft and Master Mason.

In 1838, the Grand Master of the West Indies sought permission to work the Mark Degree in Lodges under his authority. He was refused to do so, his request being at variance with Section IV, Chapter 1 of the Laws and Constitutions.

The Mark Degree in Scotland was eventually assumed into the authority of the newly formed Supreme Grand Chapter of Royal Arch Scotland in 1817. There is no record of the Mark Degree being worked between 1800 and 1817. It must be mentioned, however, that around the year 1805, The Early Grand Encampment of Ireland began to issue Charters in Scotland and the *Mark Degree* was one of the Degrees in the *Early Grand Rite*. Masonic historians have dealt elsewhere with the developments which arose out of the issue of the Irish Early Grand Charters. We are assured by the Very Worshipful Brother George S Draffen, Grand Librarian of the Grand Lodge of Scotland, that the Mark Degree was most certainly worked 'au coin de la cheminée', literally translated as 'in the corner of the fireplace'. In other words in secret at any friendly, sympathetic and suitable meeting place available. And this probably continued up until and around the 1850s. The Supreme Grand Royal Chapter of Scotland still exercises authority over the Mark Degree and divides that authority amicably with the Grand Lodge of Scotland.

By the middle of the 19th century Mark Masonry in England had become Nobody's Child. In 1851, however, something happened which was to lead to the foundation of our present Grand Lodge of Mark Master Masons of England and Wales and its Districts and Lodges Overseas.

Six Brethren who had been Advanced to the Mark Degree in the *Bon-Accord* Royal Arch Chapter of Aberdeen and who also at that time found themselves resident in London, decided that they wished to found a Mark Masons' Lodge there. In order that the proposed new Lodge should be a *Regular Lodge*, they applied to their Royal Arch Chapter *Bon-Accord* No. 70 in Aberdeen for a Warrant to form the *Bon-Accord Lodge of Mark Masters*. The Charter was duly granted on the 17th September, 1851 and the Lodge held its first meeting the next day when seven Candidates were advanced into Mark Masonry.

This is the story of how the Bon-Accord Lodge of Mark Masters was founded and, as already mentioned, the formation of the Bon-Accord Lodge led in the long run to the foundation of our present *Grand Lodge of Mark Master Masons.*

The path, however, was not a smooth one. Soon afterwards the Supreme Grand Royal Arch Chapter of Scotland repudiated the Warrant on the grounds that:

'The Aberdeen Bon-Accord Chapter had assumed to itself powers which can be exercised by the Supreme Grand Chapter alone…'

The Bon-Accord Chapter were given certain ultimatums and ordered to withdraw the Warrant immediately. They were summoned to report at the next Quarterly Communications that this had been done.

The members of Bon-Accord Chapter, without admitting their guilt, stated that they were unable to recover the Charter since the Brethren to whom the Charter was issued refused to return it. The Supreme Grand Royal Arch Chapter of Scotland subsequently recalled the Charter of the Bon-Accord Royal Arch Chapter in Aberdeen and struck it off the roll in 1855. A number of attempts were made to recover the Charter of the Bon-Accord Mark Lodge without success. Indeed the Bon-Accord Lodge of Mark Masters thrived. And the Bon-Accord Mark Lodge continues to thrive to this day, meeting at Mark Masons' Hall, St James's, London.

In 1856 seven members of United Grand Lodge and seven members of Supreme Grand Chapter of England, not all of them Mark Masons, reported to United Grand Lodge, as a Joint Committee, the following Notation: 'That the Mark Mason's Degree did *not* form part of Royal Arch Masonry, was *not* essential to Craft Masonry but it might be considered as forming 'a graceful addition to the Fellowcraft Degree'. This report was marked, 'Approved Zetland', (Earl of Zetland who was Pro Grand Master). Shortly afterwards at the March Quarterly Communications of United Grand Lodge in 1856, Brother Herbert Lloyd, Senior Grand Deacon moved the resolution…'That the Degree of Mark Mason or Mark Master is *not* at variance with the Ancient Landmarks of the Order, and that the Degree be an addition to, and form part of, Craft Masonry; and consequently may be conferred by all Regular Warranted Lodges under such regulations as shall be prepared by the Board of General Purposes, approved and sanctioned by Grand Lodge.'

The Resolution was duly approved and carried. This democratic appreciation and conclusion created a stir and provocation. Opposition forces quickly mobilised. At the very next Quarterly Communications in June, 1856, Brother John Henderson, a former President of the Board of General Purposes moved the *Non-confirmation* of the minutes of the previous Communication which referred to the Mark Degree. He denied that the Grand Lodge had the power to make so great a Constitutional change as that of adding a new Degree to the Order. By the Act of Union it had been declared that Freemasonry consisted of *Three Degrees and no more*, excepting the Royal Arch.

Brother Aria, emphatically opposing this motion, stressed the fact that in Lodges holding allegiance to the Irish, Scottish and other Grand Lodges, it was not possible to be exalted into the Royal Arch unless the Mark Degree had first been taken. Brother Aria stated that he knew for certain that throughout the West Indies and other Colonies the Mark Degree was a necessary preliminary to Exaltation. And this was true even with certain Lodges under the English Constitution. Brother Hearn, Past Provincial Deputy Grand Master for Hampshire, considered that the Mark Degree ought to be restored to its proper position in the Craft, of which it was a component part. The Grand Master was of the opinion that it was a question for Grand Chapter rather than Grand Lodge. Seeing, however, that the Book of Constitutions called upon all Masters to declare that no man, or body of men, could make innovation in the tenets of Freemasonry, and that by the Act of Union, the Order was declared to consist of three Degrees and no more, he could not do otherwise than record his vote in favour of *Non-confirmation* of the Minutes of the previous Communications concerning the Mark Degree, (Quarterly Communications 4th June 1856). The motion for the non-confirmation of these Minutes was carried by a large majority. A crushing blow to Mark

Masonry. Within a month this setback or snub was met by the formation of *The Mark Grand Lodge* and slowly but surely nearly all the bodies conferring the Mark Degree in England came under its authority. On the 30th May 1857, a meeting of Mark Masons was held at Freemasons Tavern in response to a letter from Brother Lord Leigh. Opening the proceedings from the Chair, Brother Leigh expressed a hope that, 'Whatever the Authority under which they might profess to work, the Brethren would abstain from discussing the validity of any such authority and keep in view solely the course to be pursued for the future well-being of the Craft.'

And so by the enthusiasm and persistent efforts of four Mark Lodges — The Northumberland and Berwick Lodge in Newcastle upon Tyne, The Royal Cumberland Lodge, Bath, the Old Kent Lodge, London and the Bon-Accord Lodge, London — a Grand Lodge of Mark Masons came into being. Lord Leigh was the first Grand Master.

The new Grand Lodge met with plenty of opposition. The Bon-Accord Mark Lodge No. 7 was the leading force and strength behind the formation of Grand Mark Lodge. It was not, however, deemed legitimate in the eyes of the Supreme Grand Chapter of Scotland who seethingly spoke of it as, 'Born in sin and shapen in iniquity' — the exact phraseology which, in those days, would have been used to describe a beautiful baby born out of wedlock.

In spite of this and many other trials the English Grand Mark Lodge prospered. In spite also of the awkward position in which it found itself in relation to the Scottish Grand Lodge which continued to warrant new Mark Lodges in the North of England and which in 1870 created Lancashire a Provincial Grand Mark District with its own Provincial Grand Master.

Happily and thankfully an agreement was entered into by the two Grand Lodges and ever since 1878 a Grand Lodge of Mark Master Masons of England and Wales and Dominions and Dependencies of the British Crown, now called *Grand Lodge of Mark Master Masons of England and Wales and its Districts and Lodges Overseas*, has been the sole ruler of the Mark Degree in the regions embraced by English Masonry.

The previously referred to Travelling Lodge of Cheshire known as the Travelling Lodge of Ashton-under-Lyne which had also in 1857 assumed Grand Lodge status and named itself 'The Honourable United Grand Lodge of Mark Master Masons of the Ashton-under-Lyne District', voluntarily wound itself up in 1899 and applied to the Grand Lodge of Mark Master Masons, England for a Warrant to meet under the name of Ashton District TI Mark Lodge, under which name it still operates today.

The documented history and development of the Grand Lodge of Mark Master Masons in England, Wales and its Districts and Lodges Overseas is in fact the veritable tale of 'a stone which was rejected possessing merits unknown and which ultimately became the headstone of an illustrious and esteemed structure'.

Summary

The Degree of Mark Master Mason as it is today. In England the Mark Degree is governed by the Grand Lodge of Mark Master Masons of England, Wales and its Districts and Lodges Overseas. It is open to Master Masons in Craft Masonry but is *not* a prerequisite for the Royal Arch. The Worshipful Master of a Mark Lodge should have served as the Master of a Craft Lodge but unlike the Royal Arch, a dispensation can be obtained for a Brother who is yet a Master Mason in the Craft but who has not reached the Master's Chair. He will be asked to declare in open Mark Lodge that it is his intention to do so.

In Scotland the Mark Degree is generally conferred by a Craft Lodge but may with equal legality be bestowed by a Royal Arch Chapter. The form varies considerably, some bodies being content with bare essentials and others working a ceremony similar to that of England.

In Ireland as in Scotland the Mark Degree is a prerequisite for Royal Arch Masonry. It is conferred by the Chapter usually in a separate room.

Consequently a Certificate of the Grand Lodge of Scotland or Ireland may be accepted in England as evidence that a Brother is a Mark Master Mason but *not* that he is an Installed Master in the Mark Degree. In Scotland this qualification is given to Companions of the Royal Arch on attaining the First of the Chairs in their Chapters.

Finally to conclude this section on the origin, brief history and development of the Mark Degree, I cannot find a better way of doing so than to quote some words written by the late Worshipful Brother Douglas Knoop, a well-known and much respected author of Masonic publications in the mid-20th century who described the…'Bridge between Operative and Speculative (Mark) Masonry as largely resting in Scotland at the operative end, in England at the speculative end'.

We have crossed that bridge with firmly planted and unwavering steps to what I hope is a better understanding of what we know of these origins and our development.

Duties of the Officers

Introduction

The Mark Degree, superb in its content, needs the interest, dedication and earnest involvement of the Master and his Officers if the ritual of the Lodge is to be communicated impeccably to the members of the Lodge and in particular to the Candidate during the ceremony of his advancement. The ceremony is for everyone to enjoy. For the Candidate it has to be meaningful, memorable, gratifying, and perhaps reveal first indications why the Degree is known as 'The Friendly Degree'.

The symbolism is beautiful and teaches, among other things, that we should not try to obtain that to which we are not entitled. Also that the merit of a piece of painstaking work cast aside by others as worthless may afterwards become noteworthy and creditable. 'The Stone which the Builders rejected, possessing merits to them unknown, ultimately became the Headstone of the Building'.

There are, as well we know, highly dramatic elements in the ritual. The Officers of the Lodge need to be sensitively aware and constantly on guard how they enact their roles if the symbolism is to retain its dignity and the teachings are to be passed on to the Candidate. Just one officer, absent without warning or lacking in preparation, can spoil the icing on the cake, even when the cake itself stays wholesome.

The qualities expected of each officer as well as certain duties will be appraised in turn. Scrutinising each role with a critical eye we become aware of certain recurring shortcomings. Some frank and forthright comments will be necessary from time to time. Such comments and recommendations are of course made in good faith. In the Mark Degree we are seeking the highest standards. It would be wrong to expect the Worshipful Master and his Officers to be ready-made models of poise and diction, fountains of knowledge, experts in communication. They seldom are. If, however, they judge fairly any criticisms and act wisely to implement suggestions made, then the standard of working in the Lodge can only improve. The author has learned much from observing many Brethren from many Lodges.

'Man seldom improves when he only has himself to copy after'
Alexander Pope

THE WORSHIPFUL MASTER

Every Mark Master should read carefully the 'Address' given to him on the night of his installation. It is a challenging job description which places much responsibility on the skill and ability with which he manages the affairs of the Lodge. Whether he likes it or not, he is put under the microscope by all members of his Lodge. What he does and how he does it is being carefully observed. He is in fact leading by example.

Before listing some of the desirable qualities we might expect of a good Master it is worth while at this early stage to make special mention of two habitual weaknesses. Firstly, the Master does not speak loudly enough to be heard by all members of his Lodge. And, strange though it may seem, he is seldom told about this. Once aware of the fact, the Master can increase his volume and this is aided by diaphragmatic breathing which in turn makes for easier voice projection. To ensure the correct skill, lie on your back and breathe deeply. In this position you can only breathe diaphragmatically. Now that you have the feeling, practise it standing up. It makes for relaxed throat muscles and avoids voice strain. And you will be heard!

The second major weakness of the Master is that he leaves the serious learning of the ritual until too late. As the day of the meeting approaches he does a magnificent job of memorising his words. And just as often as not he proves himself word perfect in Lodge.

Sadly, however, he has probably sacrificed communicating the beauty and significance of the ritual for remembered words. If the Master begins the serious study of his work when he reaches the Junior Warden's Chair, he will have a good two years' applied but non-hurried learning. His role will come naturally and the words will flow easily. He can then direct his energies to getting through to the Candidate and fulfilling the true objective of the Ceremony. The quality of intended expression should not give way to the act of remembering. The overall effect on his Officers and Members of his Lodge will be instructive and be passed on.

As a good and well-intentioned Mark Mason and leader of his Lodge the Master will be wishing to mark well by demonstrating additional qualities of his leadership.

CONFIDENCE. This quality goes hand in glove with knowledge. In other words a man who 'knows his stuff' is likely to be a confident man. More reason to start learning early. Poise and self assurance seldom just happen. They are the result of application and planning. However, in spite of all this you may wonder why, on the night, you have tremendous butterflies in the tummy. Be glad you have them. 'Butterflies' is the price we pay for being a racehorse and not a carthorse. It means we are sensitive to the obligation or duty that goes with communicating to groups. For example, the great Sarah Bernhardt said to a young actress who told her she never had 'butterflies' — 'My dear when you develop more talent you will have.' The nervousness you have is needed to give that little bit of extra energy.

APPLICATION OR HARD WORK. Nothing worth while was ever achieved without great effort, well, at least a reasonable amount of time and application, depending on how great or small your goals are. In addition, if you really enjoy what you are doing then the work is not so hard after all and you win both ways. Don't be misled by the aphorism, 'It will be all right on the night.' There is no substitute for endeavour.

ENTHUSIASM. This quality is a sort of controlled excitement and enjoyment. If the Master is an enthusiast then everyone around him will be infected and reflect his pleasure in the successful activities of the Lodge. A good Mason has a zest for life and living. In this way he makes a good student of human nature and understands better why we act as we do. The Mark Degree in particular manifests much friendliness. This is due perhaps to the vital lessons of its teachings which continue to grow more meaningful as we grow older.

CHARISMA. This ancient Greek word now much in current usage indicates a type of authority which motivates others to want to do the will of their leader. This means he has to be liked and preferably liked a lot. When a Master shows genuine interest in the members of his Lodge, they in turn will show interest in him and wish to support him. It is what Professor William James, the noted psychologist, called the 'Like begets Like Principle'. Know the names of the members of your Lodge and, where and when appropriate, the names of their wives. A number of Lodges now print a list which is an excellent custom. Be accessible. Don't restrict your company to a special group or clique. Never miss the opportunity to give praise to somebody for a job well done. Avoid criticism assiduously. This includes the so-called 'constructive criticism'. The Master is above all this. Should a Brother make a hash of his assignment — it happens to us all, he will be feeling very low. Most especially if he is in the early days of his Masonic career. A sincere word of encouragement from the Master will do wonders, not only for the Brother's morale but also for the Master's image and reputation.

HIGH STANDARDS. It has been written that mediocrity is the contagious bane of modern-day society. Anything goes, provided it works reasonably well and is acceptable. Whether this is true or not, mediocrity has no place in Masonic practice. A good Master will strive to excel, just as the professional athlete will wish to place the bar for his high jump a little higher than he has ever achieved before. There will always be highs and lows in achievement. The effort, however, is always recognised as well as the success. And herein lies the hallmark of the professional who says to himself — 'Give me a job to do again and I will try to do it even better.' Success is just as contagious as mediocrity.

KNOWLEDGE. Read books. Visit other Lodges. Be a good listener. Be happy and prepared to learn from every possible source including those junior to you in length of service and status. Ralph Waldo Emerson wrote in one of his famous essays:
'Every man I meet is my superior in some way or other and in that way I can learn from him.' Join the Correspondence Circle of the Quatuor Coronati Lodge. For a very modest sum you will receive Masonic literature on a regular basis, each year a bound volume containing papers on varied Masonic subjects written by the finest and most erudite Masonic brains in the world which will soon build into a useful Masonic reference library. All this in addition to having welcome access to the greatest and most extensive source of Masonic information in the world.

SENSE OF HUMOUR. Have fun and enjoy what you are doing. Stay calm in the face of adversity. Never be surprised when events do not run smoothly or according to plan. The Tyler does not turn up; the Candidate has not brought his MM's apron; the Senior Deacon has lost his voice. Even the VSL can go missing, usually borrowed by another Lodge using the same storage area. Don't panic! Do the very best you can in the circumstances. You can't do more. You will probably have a laugh afterwards. So why not give a smile now. The important aim is to prevent wear and tear on your nervous system. Get yourself a copy of Brother Rudyard Kipling's Poem, *If*, and add years to your life.

PUNCTUALITY. A strict rule! The Lodge should be opened precisely at the time stated on the Summons. Both Master and Director of Ceremonies should agree this and make sure it happens. The same strict rule applies to Lodge of Instruction, a rehearsal or committee meeting.

PRECEPT AND EXAMPLE. Men are influenced more by personal example than by precept. The Master is unlikely to sermonise or preach. What he does, however, in the Temple and away from it, will be copied. It was stated in Roman Times — 'Precept is like to a message writ in the sands. The tide comes and washes it out. Example is like unto a graving in the rock which will remain long after the message is forgotten.'

THE WARDENS

At the Installation Ceremony, both Wardens are congratulated on their appointments, 'inasmuch as the Wardenship is a necessary step to higher office'. It follows then that the high standard of qualities and skills demanded of the Master apply equally to both Wardens. The plain truth is that the office of Warden is often not given the attention needed to support fully the efforts of the Master. One wonders why it is that there tend to be instances of absenteeism among Wardens in the Mark Degree that could not be tolerated in the Craft. Furthermore, it is not unusual to see the 'little blue book' being read hurriedly before the Lodge is opened. A last minute look to ease the conscience perhaps. Usually futile. The criticism may sound harsh but it is not exaggerated. Part of the problem is, I am sure, that the Wardens do not have enough work to do. So they leave their preparation too late, perhaps even to the night before the meeting. And the preparation itself has probably been somewhat cursory or casual, and is soon forgotten. Sadly the relatively little they then have to do is often below acceptable standards. For example, the Junior Warden does not bother to check out the Inner Guard's name, be he the regular officer or a stand-in. Whether he needs it or not, the 'little blue book' is placed on his pedestal as a safeguard. Such books openly displayed in Lodge project the wrong image. When closing the Lodge accordingly it is assuring and well received if the JW announces the date of the next meeting. His special duty in the Ceremony of Advancement has to be carefully thought out and rehearsed in his own mind and handled with propriety. Even a brief rehearsal before the meeting will pay dividends in preserving the dignity of the whole Ceremony.

In similar fashion the Senior Warden also has to enact his contribution with much delicacy. The importance of a brief rehearsal of this particular scene cannot be too strongly emphasised. To be fair, it has to be said that the SW also places his 'little blue book' on the pedestal but in his case it is hidden by the 'Wickets'. He later discovers that he can't read the small print from the standing position. If not properly prepared he has to pick up the book and read it in full view. Perhaps his most common fault is that he persistently confuses the 'Opening' terminology with the 'Closing' terminology.

The recommendations which follow are made in good faith and founded on critical observations made over a span of many years:

ENDEAVOUR to make a daily advancement in Masonic knowledge;

READ the Address to the Wardens;

KNOW your ritual absolutely word perfect and set an important example to the other officers of the Lodge;

READ and study the Address to the Master; begin a programme of planned study in readiness for the Master's Chair;

REGULARLY attend. Inform the Master in good time of any known possible absence;

PAY meticulous attention to detail. For example know the Inner Guard's name, and ensure the candidate's apron and jewel are readily accessible, the apron strap has been adjusted and there is a Mark Token for each Candidate.

In conclusion there is one more way in which the Wardens can prove themselves of considerable help to the Master and of benefit to the Lodge. There is a need for education and enlightenment in the form of lectures on the Mark Master Masons' Degree and the Mark Degree Tracing Board. This is too often neglected when there are so many Candidates awaiting their Advancement Ceremony. The Wardens could take on the responsibility of organising such lectures in 'Catechetical Form' under the guidance of the Master and the Director of Ceremonies. This is a most effective means of communication since it involves the welcome participation of Lodge members.

The predominant message to both Wardens is 'Give the high office of Wardenship the attention and respect it deserves, attend regularly and support the Worshipful Master in all aspects of governing the Lodge, to achieve by your assistance the highest standards of the ritual.'

OVERSEERS

The Office of Overseer and the value of his role tends to be underestimated. The Master would do well to give all three of them sincere appreciation for work well done. Each Overseer should be reminded frequently that he is a Principal Officer of the Lodge and therefore committed to regular attendance. It is highly important that whenever possible an Overseer gives ample notice of intended absence so that a substitute can be appointed. Sometimes it is difficult to find in Lodge a Brother qualified enough to step into the Overseer's Chair and it is not unknown for a visitor to be asked to fill the vacancy. There tends to be a fairly high incidence of absenteeism among Overseers. This may be because the Overseer is unaware of just how important his job is. Hence the recommendation that the Master pays just that little bit more attention to his Overseers. All three have much more to do than a hasty first glance of the ritual would indicate. They are also involved in certain physical manoeuvres which require skilful handling and resourcefulness. For example, the correct examination procedure and handling of the Stones. A more natural intonation of the voice is needed when expressing judgement as to the workmanship and suitability. Then there is the manner with which each Overseer presents himself to the Master Overseer when he calls a Council concerning the KS. Short of a rehearsal, this part of the ritual and certain parts yet to be mentioned have to be seriously studied and carefully learned. Sadly this is seldom the case. Yet it is all detailed in the ritual. There is the Master's interrogation of each Overseer concerning the missing KS. Here we have yet another example where the detailed guidance clearly set out in the 'blue book' is for some reason disregarded. The result is a version of well-written dialogue and clearly explained gestures being simulated in a different manner at each and every ceremony. It should be emphasised that there is a correct way how and when to salute and a correct way for the Overseer to take the plan and study it before handing it back to the WM with the appropriate comments.

Practise the physical actions and movements with accurate deliberation. Make haste slowly. The Opening of the Lodge is yet another good illustration of this. When the WM calls you by your Office title, take time to move clockwise to the prescribed end of your pedestal and face East. Don't forget to commence your reply with 'to guard that gate', when the WM asks you '…why etc'. A common fault of omission. Then with the same precise deliberation return to your place. It is to be hoped that the WM will give you time to do this before continuing with the next one of his questions. So, to recapitulate, some recommendations to the Overseers:

> You are a Principal Officer committed to regular attendance;
> Give the earliest notice possible of any absence;
> The 'little blue book' placed on the pedestal is inept;
> Study carefully what is expected of you and use your normal speaking voice to communicate in a meaningful way. Pay special attention to the significant actions and procedures in keeping with your role;
> Prepare your activities well in advance of the meeting.

Repeat your ritual until you know that you really know that you know it. Never miss the opportunity to hold a rehearsal, however brief, when the opportunity presents itself. Keep constantly in mind that by doing a good job you are setting an impeccable example to all those who follow you. And this will be passed on.

THE SECRETARY

The Lodge Secretary is responsible for the effective administration of the Lodge. He is therefore a Brother who is selected rather than recruited. He should be skilled in both verbal and written communications. In most instances he will be a Past Master of the Order but not necessarily so.

It is no secret that he is the 'Éminence grise' of the lodge. In other words the Power behind the Master's Chair. He does not abuse this power and is ever conscious that the new Worshipful Master is dependent on his help and guidance.

To assist him in his many tasks he should have an assistant who can relieve him of such duties as recording 'apologies', and the dining arrangements.

In response to a series of questions directed to Provincial Grand Secretaries it would appear that the most common weakness of Lodge Secretaries is 'late returns' which can cause problems down the line.

The Lodge Secretary should be invited to participate in the Lodge Ceremonies from time to time. For example, the explanation of the Tracing Boards, various Charges and indeed the Catechetical Lectures. Should the Lodge Secretary not be a Past Master, it is important that, whilst engaged in his important duties, he does not lose any seniority in progressing towards the Master's Chair.

THE TREASURER

The Treasurer, as we know, is not appointed by the Worshipful Master, but is proposed, seconded and voted for in open Lodge every year.

His important function is much more specialised today than that of a simple book-keeper. In addition to keeping the accounts in a regular and systematic manner, he has to sign cheques on behalf of the Lodge. He has therefore to keep a close check on the cash flow. He also has a forecasting job to do by foreseeing future expenses and making his recommendations accordingly. However conscientious and competent, this Officer, who is in charge of collected funds, can only be as efficient as members of his Lodge allow him to be.

He is looking for one hundred per cent co-operation from Lodge members that payment of Lodge subscriptions are made immediately they become due.

When this happens, the Lodge Treasurer is able to spend more time giving creative thought on how to control and reduce expenses, which in turn is of benefit to the Lodge funds and Lodge members alike.

As in the case of the Lodge Secretary, the Lodge Treasurer should be encouraged to take part in Lodge ritual practice. Neither should a good Lodge Treasurer be held back from his rightful progression towards the Master's Chair, should he so desire.

THE CHAPLAIN

The Chaplain should be a carefully selected Past Master of the Lodge, preferably chosen for the devout nature of his character as well as for other personal qualities.

A good speaking voice, loud enough to be heard in Lodge, and a clear diction would be considered definite assets. And of course regular attendance is most important.

The duties of the Chaplain are often underestimated. He has a lot of important work to do in the Ceremony of Advancement. It is for this reason that we strongly recommend to him that *he makes use of his own personal VSL* rather than read from the ritual book. In addition to projecting a more reverend and pious image, it is much more acceptable that he does not set the wrong example by reading the ritual book in Lodge.

In the Opening and Closing Ceremonies he is expected to commit the prayers to memory. However, often with advancing years the memory is not as reliable as we would wish it, in which case the prayers would be equally acceptable if read from notes in his personal VSL.

THE REGISTRAR OF MARKS

The Office of Registrar of Marks is usually filled by an experienced Past Master of the Lodge. He is responsible for keeping a Register of Lodge members and of their chosen Marks.

During the Ceremony of Advancement he will offer the Candidate a choice of usually three Marks which he has devised. If he wishes he may use the Masonic Cypher or, more simply, his own ingenuity with the letters of the alphabet and the Candidate's initials.

These Marks he will prepare in advance and place them on his table where he is situated on the right hand of the Secretary.

The Marks must be made up of straight lines but in no way should they contain the Triangle. Some Candidates find it difficult to choose a Mark or fail to recognise immediately a Mark which is particularly well suited to them. The Registrar should be prepared to advise the Candidate accordingly. As with other specialist Officers of the Lodge, the Registrar of Marks should not be ignored or precluded from being asked to participate from time to time in the Lodge Ceremonies — involvement in the Catechismal Lectures and the Tracing Board, for example.

THE DIRECTOR OF CEREMONIES

The Director of Ceremonies should essentially be a Past Master. Many Past Masters feel that they would like to hold office as Director of Ceremonies of their Lodge. It is a challenging Office not without a touch of glamour and excitement. Regrettably, however, only a few ever meet with the strict criteria of qualities and skills needed for the job. Rank, knowledge and length of service are not enough. Each and every year the Director of Ceremonies has to win the confidence of a new team of Officers and motivate them to give of their best. He should be genuinely interested in people. A friendly personality is requisite to the Office, as is an engaging smile. He needs essentially to be expert in communication and have a passion to persuade. He doesn't give orders but reminds people of what they know already. Alexander Pope in his *Essay on Criticism* writes:

'Men must be taught as if you taught them not, And things unknown proposed as things forgot'

A good Director of Ceremonies never stops learning. He builds up a tremendous reserve power of knowledge which makes him cleverer than most other people but he never ever makes a point of letting them know it. How widespread the following anecdote or conundrum is generally known is not easy to say but it is still very much worth while recording it here. A Brother once asked his friend the question, 'What is the difference between a Director of Ceremonies and an Regimental Sergeant Major?' 'Not a lot,' replied his friend, 'but I do know it is sometimes possible to negotiate with a Regimental Sergeant Major.' An amusing little story perhaps! But somewhere here lurks a grain of truth which should not be passed over lightly by many who hold this important Office. Shakespeare speaks of the proud man, dressed in a little brief authority, being capable of such actions before high heaven as would make the angels weep.

The Director of Ceremonies should be constantly aware that he is teaching and influencing others by example: his bearing, his voice, the respectful manner with which he treats all the Brethren both in the Temple and at the Festive Board. He has many, many duties to perform. When he wishes to make certain rules concerning the harmony or smooth running of a Ceremony, he should state such rules clearly and gain acceptance from others that they agree. For example, the matter of prompting in Lodge can easily get out of hand. So the rule is, 'No prompting to be done except by the Director of Ceremonies or his assistant.' Another rule is, 'Only the Immediate Past Master will prompt the Worshipful Master.'

He will also demonstrate traditional practices such as the drill movements of how one positions the Wand when saluting as a Mark Master Mason. Each Director of Ceremonies will usually have his own interpretation of certain practices and his own style of working them; all, of course, in strict accordance with Lodge tradition and Masonic usage. His job will be a lot easier if he makes this clear and wins the confidence as well as the agreement of the Master and his Officers beforehand.

His influential and exalted Office is, however, rationally tempered by the knowledge that it is not an obligatory appointment and that the Worshipful Master need not appoint a Director of Ceremonies should he not wish to do so. In practice this seldom happens since the services of a good Director of Ceremonies are invaluable if the Lodge is to maintain predetermined standards of efficiency and the involvement of all the Brethren. As a general rule, when the Worshipful Master himself is new to his job, both he and his Officers feel more secure and confident under the guidance of a good Director of Ceremonies.

Having read and mentally absorbed the criteria of the qualities needed to become a good Director of Ceremonies and you are still determined to make a bid for this Office you may be prompted to ask the question, 'How long does it usually take to become a good Director of Ceremonies?' The answer is…'a lifetime'.

THE DEACONS

The duties of the Deacons may be specified as a highly important function in the Mark Degree. They have the responsibility of conducting the Candidate through his Ceremonies as a Mark Man and as a Mark Master Mason. It is true that the Senior Deacon does most of the work but do not underestimate a good Junior Deacon who will know the work just as well, in case of absence. The Office of Deacon, however, has an excellent attendance record. Most good Deacons have begun to prepare for the job when they were Stewards. This sort of dedication and enthusiasm is manifested by the way they help each other and work as a team.

The main weakness is their floorwork and positioning during the Ceremony of Advancement. It is also desirable that the Deacon is heard in Lodge. We have already discussed the importance of voice projection and good articulation. The way in which the Deacons carry and make use of their Wands as badges of their Office is an aspect of the ritual which is rarely discussed. But let us analyse first of all the floorwork. The problem is not what to do, but where and how to do it. So there is no need to go into great detail about what to do since it is there in the ritual and already second nature. Where and how to do it would not be a problem if it was possible to have more rehearsals. Failing this, as you study your 'blue book', take a piece of A4 paper, lay it in front of you and mark the relative positions of the WM, the SW and the JW. Mark in also the positions of the Overseers' Pedestals. And for good measure the position of the Secretary's table. Now where you are at or where you will be at any given moment will be relative to those stated positions in Lodge. Reading the 'blue book' from the beginning of the Ceremony of Advancement, trace your movements and mark the paper accordingly: when the candidate is flanked by both Deacons on entry into the Lodge; at the first perambulation when the SD leaves the JD in the north-west. The SD will in due course note his position relative to the JW's Pedestal, that is to say, slightly to the East and facing West. Work completed, he proceeds to the SW's Pedestal, slightly to the South and facing North. The SD should continue his duties throughout the ritual, step by step, making his own private notes concerning his position in Lodge and what he is doing relative to the dialogue. There is no need to spell out here what is already well written in the ritual. The fact is, however, we tend to ignore the ritual and copy the habits of those who have preceded us. This is wrong. Let the Deacons who are reading these words get it right for themselves by a carefully detailed study. And should anyone wish to copy another Deacon's example then let them also check it by reference to the ritual. An important instance is the 'advance to the Pedestal in due form'. This manoeuvre ought to be carefully studied and planned. A great advantage is that which is planned carefully on paper becomes a mental fixture which can be tried out and consolidated in Lodge by getting there a little early before the meeting. And it is something you can do on your own if needs be. Additional benefits will be mentioned in a later section styled 'The Written Rehearsal'.

Concerning Wands, it is written in the Preface to the Mark Ritual that Deacons should not carry Wands when discharging duties which are not ceremonial. This much needed amendment was formalised in 1988 when up to that time the unfortunate Deacon had to struggle in a very ungainly manner to distribute voting slips with his left hand whilst holding his Wand in his right. There were other like duties such as the ballot box, carrying the Minute Book from the Secretary's desk to the WM for signing, and one has occasionally witnessed the scene of the Deacon attempting to salute the WM as well, before and after. It is probable that the discipline of carrying the Wand dates back from earlier times when two Very Eminent Directors of Ceremony in Craft Masonry laid down most emphatically that the Wand was a badge of office and authority which must never be separated from the holder. A badge of office and dignity it certainly is, but the amendment is still a very practical one and the Wand need not now be carried for such tasks as mentioned, including the alms collection and indeed gathering in the Working Plans.

Bernard E Jones in his *Freemasons' Guide and Compendium* writes:

'The Wand has had its place in all ceremonial rites throughout the ages and has been carried by kings and others in authority as the sign and token of office and importance, of power, strength and government. History shows that the person's power or right to act is by virtue of his holding or carrying the Wand, and from this the Lodge Officer — be he Director of Ceremonies,

Deacon, or Steward entrusted with temporary office — learns that he, too, derives his authority from the actual carrying of a Wand which was placed in his hands by the Master of the Lodge. His Wand is an emblem of power, dignity, and significance deriving from ancient days.'

Many mentions are made of wands or staffs or rods in Roman and Greek history, and the Bible. All denote power and leadership. The sceptre is one of the many forms of Wand. So why do most Deacons debase this authority, this dignity, by using their Wands as a pointer to facilitate all sorts of ordinary and commonplace actions or functions? For example, correcting a Candidate's feet posture and movements or detailing the explanation of the Tracing Board, to name only two. The custom of bearing the Wand is a tradition which gives us the stewardship of an unbroken link with ceremonial behaviour and observances over a period of thousands of years. Deacons should get together with Directors of Ceremonies to discuss and decide comportment and specific practice concerning the bearing of Wands. It is an issue where guidance from Grand Lodge would be of tremendous assistance both now and in the future. There is a widespread saying about Deacons — 'You can always tell a good future Master by the quality of his work on the floor as a Deacon.' And there are many instances to indicate that this belief is perfectly true.

THE ORGANIST

Brother Organist is a welcome asset to his Lodge. His skills in music are always a delight to listen to and they add tremendously to the success and enjoyment of a Ceremony. He is very much missed if he fails to attend. Fortunately this is seldom the case. He is usually a quiet, unobtrusive stalwart who is always there when needed. For these reasons we should never take him for granted. And like every other Officer of the Lodge he deserves praise for work well done. The D of C would do well to discuss with him how best to make even greater use of his talents. For example, a small choir of three strong voices seated near the organ would help considerably to give a much needed booster to the 'Mark Masters' Chant'. If the Lodge happens to be a 'Chanting' Lodge, an approach like this is strongly recommended. As a general rule, the chants are delivered in a dismally half-hearted manner and do nothing to enhance the Ceremony whatsoever. The Organist with his small choir can make the world of a difference.

There are occasions too, when the Organist would enjoy being asked to participate in the Lectures — the Tracing Board for example.

THE INNER GUARD

When the Inner Guard is invested he is told that his position is within the entrance of the Lodge. His duty is to report to the WM when Brethren claim admission, to admit Mark Masons on proof, receive Candidates in due form, and obey the commands of the Junior Warden. The Office of Inner Guard has an interesting history with the duties allied to those of the Tyler who would alert him on the approach of a stranger or possible marauder. He in turn would inform the Warden or Master. In those earliest days he was called the door-keeper and very likely to be the most junior entered apprentice of the Lodge and armed with a trowel. He was later called a Garder or Gard. Around 1814 Grand Lodge gave official recognition to the Office of Inner Guard and some five years later in 1819 approved and authorised the Inner Guard's Jewel of Crossed Swords. Today he is an Assistant Officer of the Lodge and makes a positive contribution in the opening and closing of the Lodge as well as the Advancement Ceremony of a new Brother. As such, it is his first opportunity as an Officer in his own right to attract favourable attention to himself by his bearing, a loud and clear authoritative voice heard by all members from the door of the Lodge to the Master's Chair. He will of course assure himself that the JW knows his name and that his Mallet and Chisel are conveniently placed in Lodge for his use. When addressing the Tyler during Ceremonies he should take care that what he has to say is heard by all the members of the Lodge. Should the JW on occasions give him wrong instructions, for example during the ritual of Opening and Closing of the Lodge, he will do what he knows to be correct.

It is the Inner Guard who first receives the Candidate on his entry into the Lodge. Before doing so, however, he has to advance to the WM to give him the PG and the pw on behalf of the Candidate. Duty performed, he returns directly to his station and stands to order with the H SIGN. This part of the Ceremony carried out as it should be can create a dramatic sense of expectancy of the Ceremony to follow. This seldom happens. The WM tends to rush things and begins to issue further instructions before the Inner Guard gets back to his station and stands to order.

It is to be hoped that having read this comment the WM will be careful to wait until the Inner Guard has reached his station and is standing properly to order before continuing with the Ceremony.

The actual reception of the Candidate within the door of the Lodge needs a little more careful planning. The Inner Guard would do well to discuss the procedure with the Deacons and if possible for all three to have a quick practice how to arrange themselves competently in their correct positions. This will allow the Inner Guard to carry out his important task more effectively, once again setting an impressive scene for the Ceremony to follow. The importance and quality of the Inner Guard's well thought out involvement especially at the beginning of the Ceremony should not be underestimated. No less than William Shakespeare alluded to, 'their exits and their entrances' as being the hallmark of professionals.

THE STEWARDS

The Steward in a Lodge has his foot on the first rung of a ladder which if climbed judiciously should lead him to the Master's Chair. The Office of Steward should never be looked upon as a sinecure. There is plenty for him to do. Each Lodge has its own customs but in general a good Steward is happy to be of help in a wide range of activities in the Lodge from arranging the layout of the furniture to serving wine, with much decorum, at the top table. In these modern times, the duties of the Steward as addressed to him at the Installation Ceremony are scarcely now relevant except in the most general of terms. He should, however, ensure that Lodge visitors are being well looked after and that no Brother is left on his own which is, of course, automatic and fundamental to Mark Masonry.

The office of Steward may last during a period of several years. This is an important time to the Steward for his own personal development. Abraham Lincoln, as a struggling young lawyer, wrote about his own concept of seeking fame and fortune — 'I will prepare myself and the opportunity will come.' If a Steward will take time to know the work of the Inner Guard, learn the work of the Deacons, it can be a shortcut to distinction. It is certain that one of those Officers will on an occasion be unable to attend. And the Steward who can take his place will inevitably draw favourable attention to himself and of course gain tremendous self satisfaction on his achievement. He should let the Director of Ceremonies know of his willingness to participate in Lodge Ceremonies, eg the Working Tools and Catechismal Lectures. Several Stewards have been known to draw up their own personal development plan. It is a means of keeping themselves on track and assists them also to make a daily advancement in Masonic knowledge.

The future well-being of the Lodge and the continuity of high standards of ritual are very much dependent on the motivation of the Stewards and of course other junior members of the Lodge, not yet in Office, who might also wish to prepare themselves for future responsibilities. All of them should be given sincere appreciation for work well done. And if, in addition, they were to ask themselves and give positive answers to the following two questions, 'Why am I doing this specific thing? What do I hope to achieve by doing so?', this will assist them to choose specific goals and eventually to excel themselves on every rung of the ladder.

The Cornucopia, ancient Greek symbol of abundance, and emblematic of the horn which could be filled with whatever the owner wished, is a well-chosen jewel for the Office of Steward.

The Tyler

The history of the Tyler in Freemasonry is much varied and abounds in a myriad of theories. Since there are many books on the subject for the reader to discover, we will settle for something simple and reasonably logical. History informs us that castles, as fortified structures, had their watch towers. There was at least one sentinel whose duty it was to observe and to alert a warning to the commander below. Despite the importance of his function, the roof sentinel was not considered a person of any great consequence — rather like a night watchman in a factory or warehouse.

In the Middle Ages, as well as masons there were also makers of tiles for roofing, known as tilers. They were itinerant and they accompanied the migratory masons to perform their share of the construction work by covering the buildings. The tilers were of much lower status than the master mason who was an architect, quantity surveyor and builder rolled into one. Sentinels or guards would be therefore selected from among the less important tilers or tylers. Duly named, the tradition lives on. This explanation, will, without doubt, prove somewhat too simple for those academics who have made serious and detailed study of the origins of the Tyler. Serious researchers have produced convincing evidence that the true origin was with the Knights Templar. As stated earlier, there is a wealth of literature concerning the Tyler and his evasive origins, more than enough to satisfy the curiosity of the most interested of Brethren.

In Freemasonry the Tyler is the outer guard and his duty was to keep off all cowans and intruders to Masonry, for which purpose he is armed with a drawn sword. He has the equally important duty to ensure that the Candidate is properly prepared. This is much more than just the physical preparation of seeing the Candidate properly clothed and so on. It entails talking with the Candidate, and counselling him so that he is able to meet the demands of his Ceremony with confidence and healthy anticipation. We are now discussing a job that requires knowledge, much Masonic experience and skills in communication. Bernard Jones states in his *Freemasons' Guide*, 'The old French Lodges recognised the Tyler's office as one of the greatest importance, being convinced that as he was one of the earliest of the lodge officers to have contact with the Candidate he needed to be most carefully chosen for the task.' He also quotes from a French publication dated 1828, 'The greatest honour a Master can confer on a Brother is to make him Tyler, because not only his own secrets but those of the whole Lodge are depending on him.'

The Tyler continued to have other important tasks to perform. He would deliver Summonses by hand. He was often called upon to prepare the Summons, and in some Lodges to be responsible for the minutes. He would draw up the Symbolic Lodge with lines of chalk on the floor of the Lodge and supervise the junior entered apprentices whose job it was to erase the chalk marks when the Lodge was closed. He was paid for his services one shilling and sixpence for each meeting. This custom persists today. In the larger conurbations Lodges engage experienced and highly recommended Past Masters as their Tylers and pay them an annual fee for their services. Such Tylers are very well qualified and can be relied upon to carry out their duties with the minimum of supervision.

In the Provinces and rural areas, the office of Tyler is often a progressive one carried out by an actual member of the Lodge. He is usually the Senior Steward who is promoted to Tyler and from there moves on to Inner Guard. As an Officer of the Lodge he is not of course paid for his services. And as a relatively inexperienced Officer his work should be closely supervised. Errors of procedure and other mistakes should be tactfully corrected at once. This applies in particular to the preparation procedure for the 'Workmen from the Quarries with materials for the building....' The officer to supervise should be the Director of Ceremonies or his assistant if he has one. Neither should miss an opportunity to praise the inexperienced Tyler for a job well done.

Making sure the members of the Lodge sign the register is another of the Tyler's many duties. If in addition he can remind or persuade the Brethren to make their Marks after their signature, then he really is doing a fine job.

The Written Rehearsal and Commentary

The 'Written Rehearsal' is pure conjecture and supposition. It is a short treatise to draw beneficial attention to those parts of the ritual which are not usually enacted as well as they might be by the Officers of the Lodge and also to comment on certain parts of the ceremony which are praiseworthy and creditable to the Mark Ritual as a whole. The Antiquity of the Degree is well established. The Beauty and Teachings of the Degree can only be perpetuated by the dedicated efforts of those of us who are privileged to practise it. Mark Masons are not lacking in capacity but for want of some sort of guidance they may be lacking in application. The treatise, therefore, is not a criticism, but a series of guide posts aimed at pointing us in the right direction. And a mental refresher to be read just before each meeting.

It is not intended to disclose or discuss in this treatise any sensitive matters peculiar to the Degree. The reader will therefore know, without being told, to make use of his empirical knowledge from time to time, to protect its privacy. Prior to the Lodge being opened it is most reassuring to see the Stewards, early on purpose, checking general arrangements under the guidance of the D of C. These include a working plan on each of the Overseer's Pedestals as well as a Mallet and T-Square for the Master Overseer and a Mallet and Square for the Junior and Senior Overseers; a Mark Token, a Mark Apron and Jewel on the SW's Pedestal; two Kn Stools; the TB; the IG's Mallet and Chisel inside the door of the Lodge. Outside the door of the Lodge three Working Aprons and the appropriate Stones should be readily available. It is always expedient to have a Craft Apron (MM) in reserve in case the Candidate does not bring his own.

In this Lodge the Master and his Wardens process in alone. All other Officers have taken up their respective positions in Lodge. The Candles are lit and we are ready to open.

OPENING THE LODGE

The Lodge is opened with one or two hiccups. This is not unusual. The JW has forgotten the IG's name. The SW confuses the opening terminology with that of closing but corrects himself. The JO forgets to 'Guard that Gate'. Otherwise everything goes very well indeed. The Master is confident and he can be heard by all the members. He has a ready smile and welcomes both members and visitors. He produces and displays to the members the Warrant of the Lodge which is their authority from Grand Lodge to hold their meetings. Not all Lodges have their Warrants on show either temporarily on the evening of the meeting or permanently in the Temple. In which case it is necessary to produce the Warrant, and this is not always done. The Officers are responding well and are speaking up. The Overseers are moving clockwise, each to his respective position, and they are word perfect, indicating that they are well prepared. The Chaplain knows his contribution and has no need to refer to the 'book'. If he does have to refer to it then quite frankly he does not set a good enough example to others. Apart from the hiccups mentioned, (and easily remedied), the Opening has proved to be very good and as a final touch the members, taking their time with the WM, give the third part of the first Sign and discharge it in unison. Very effective!

The WM should be aware that he is the pacemaker and deliberate the sign accordingly. The IPM has now his small duty to perform to complete the Opening. He should note carefully the ritual instructions for placing the WT's on the VSL. Lodges have their own traditions and customs, but as a general rule the IPM will 'bow in, and salute out'; in other words, a court bow, arrange the WT's, then salute before returning to his Chair. A good Opening is very important since it sets the pace and the high standards for the rest of the evening.

The Ceremony of Advancement

From the moment the Tyler gives the FC Knocks, it is action stations. What follows is the important reception of the Candidate. We have already stressed the importance of this early part of the Ceremony when discussing the duties of the IG. We would reiterate, however, that the dialogue with the Tyler should be heard equally well by the members inside the Lodge. The WM having received the PG and the pw from the IG should allow him sufficient time to return to his station and stand to order with the H SIGN before resuming his instructions.

The reception of the Candidate flanked by the Deacons immediately on entering the Temple and the work of the IG is a captivating moment at the beginning of the Advancement Ceremony. It needs rehearsing, if only briefly.

It should create an atmosphere of anticipation even among those who have seen the Ceremony many times. The Deacons are now a focus of attention as they receive the Candidate in the practised manner, and position themselves correctly in front of the now closed door. This tricky little operation should be carried out with collected and unruffled calm.

It is now for the IG to summarise the Candidate's progress so far. We have no problems here. The IG knows his lines and he can be heard clearly throughout the Lodge. The Candidate is then commanded to enter on the edge of the C.

The WM demands the proofs and it is now the turn of the Deacons to play their role in the Candidate's Advancement — the Senior Deacon in particular. We get off to a faulty start here. The JD forgets to remain in the NW and begins to tag along behind the SD and the Candidate on the perambulation. He quickly realises his mistake and retreats to the NW to attend to the Kn Stool and stand facing E as instructed in the ritual. The Senior Deacon conducts the Candidate with confidence. His bearing is faultless and he carries his Wand with much dignity. The common fault at this stage is that unthinkingly he may salute the JW and the SW respectively along with the Candidate. Only the Candidate salutes. But make sure he takes the step first. And don't allow him to shuffle through it. Before asking the Candidate to salute the WM as a MM, full Signs, request him first in a low voice to stand to order as an FC. He will now find it easier to take the step and move deftly into the Signs. Otherwise he will seldom take the step and end up moving like a broken-down windmill.

During the prayer which follows, the Candidate as well as the two Deacons place the right hand over the heart. This means the Deacons have to cross their Wands over the kneeling Candidate, holding the Wands in their left hands. This is seldom done in a satisfactory manner. The Wands slip to one side, then too much to the other side in an attempt to compensate. The Deacons seem unaware, for the most part, of the slouchiness of the Wands and of the awkwardness of their overall stance. Symmetry can be achieved by knowing this and with a little extra concentration on what they are doing.

The Chaplain who is usually a carefully selected Past Master may be elderly and feel that the prayer which follows, and indeed several more prayers later in the Ceremony, are too much for him to know by heart. This is acceptable. But not the 'blue book'. The earnest suggestion is that he uses his own personal copy of the VSL. The image is reverential and pious and does not hint to others wrong ideas about using the 'book' in Lodge.

From time to time in the ritual we read, 'Omnes — SMIB'. This means exactly what it says. So let's have a more spirited response from everyone.

The SD conducts the Candidate to the Registrar's table with the same aforementioned bearing and dignity. A choice of suitable Marks for the Candidate is the responsibility of the Registrar who is also a carefully selected Past Master. He may if he wishes make use of the Masonic Cypher.

Note that the 'Mark which is aptly chosen' is communicated to the WM with the FC sign and this will be observed until much later in the Ceremony.

The WM stands when indenting the triangle around the Candidate's Mark. When designating him a Mark Man there should be a little extra emphasis on the word *Man*. And to place the Mark in the Candidate's left hand as naturally as possible, he should offer it directly to the left hand. Thus avoiding the prompt, 'No, the other hand' at this important moment of the Ceremony.

The WM should now explain clearly and unequivocally his instructions when entrusting the Candidate with the token of that rank. Time spent on a clear explanation is well invested. Later when the Signs of the Degree are demonstrated, they will be more readily understood.

With stately bearing, holding his Wand as a proud badge of office the SD conducts the Candidate to the front of the SW's Pedestal. With like dignity and ceremonial prowess reminiscent of Black Rod knocking on the door of the House of Commons, the SD knocks three times on the floor with his Wand. In reply to the SW's challenge question the SD salutes with the FC sign and gives his detailed reply in word perfect manner. None the less a small problem here!

The FC sign has been given differently from the one he has just given previously. Truly, it can be difficult holding the Wand and saluting at the same time, and one tends to do what comes easiest at that moment. The D of C should explain beforehand how he wishes the salute to be given in Lodge and demonstrate. Following this it takes only a little practice at home with the aid of a broom handle to perfect the movement.

Once again, I'm afraid, we have problems with the SW who does not know his words well enough. He gets a little confused. He has his 'book' on his Pedestal — hidden, of course, by the two Wickets. He recites and half reads what he has to say. Then a moment later he is stymied. He cannot read his 'book' from the standing position when he presents the Candidate to the WM as a Mark Man qualified for advancement etc. His LH is engaged with the Candidate and his RH with the SIGN OF F. The exact wording escapes him. But since he knows roughly what he has to say, he muddles through. An example of how, if we are not careful and attentive, the brilliance and splendour of the ritual of the Mark Degree can give way to the commonplace.

Advancing to the Pedestal in due form has to be planned beforehand, and this we have already discussed when analysing the duties of the Deacons. Gauge the correct position for the commencement of the manoeuvre, follow the instructions in the ritual to the letter, and know where the feet should be at any given moment and in which direction they should be pointing. Two Deacons and the Candidate should all three finish together, close to the WM's Pedestal. Note that the words 'long and slow' can be drawn out. And the words 'short and quick' can be given briefly and in a forcibly concise manner — an attention to detail for that little extra decorative and graphic effect.

The solemnity and the impact of the 'Obligation' is dependent on a number of factors. First of all the WM, who we assume is knowledgeable in the art of communication and is sensitive to the difference between speaking memorised words and imparting essential information in a way that will be readily understood and remembered. Meaningful communication, alas, is still not the complete answer. Candidates come in many forms. Some are nervous. Some are hard of hearing. Some may have speech impediments. Any one of those instances can easily tumble the WM off his balance and upset his cool composure. Continuous prompting and having to repeat the words to the Candidate cause him to lose the thread of what he is saying. Confusion, panic, and the memory goes. Fortunately this does not happen often. To avoid it happening at all, and to make it easier for the WM to learn and remember the words of his Address, even under stressful conditions, there is a recommended solution. Divide the complete address into short, precise phrases which not only make sense to the Candidate, but make it easier for him to remember and repeat. Be careful to avoid ambiguous phrases like, — but I shall not feel myself — quoted more frequently than you would imagine. The WM should learn the passage in this manner without deviating at all from the predetermined phrases. As he learns each phrase he should pause and mentally hear the Candidate repeat it. Once the WM has the words under his belt, so to speak, he should then begin to rehearse the passage in the standing position, showing the SIGN OF F and imagining the Candidate properly positioned before him. There is a marked difference between learning something in a seated position and then delivering it from a standing position on the night. Things are always different in front of an audience. Rehearse your stance, even the position of your right hand. In the event that you find yourself with a nervous or difficult to work with Candidate you are unlikely to be thrown off course since as you are working to a predetermined pattern you can more readily pick up the threads of your dialogue. There is a good, sound general rule to be learned here. When learning and rehearsing privately and on your own, always try to simulate the conditions you will eventually be working in.

It has to be mentioned again that the Deacons must learn to concentrate on maintaining the correct symmetry of their crossed Wands.

With the utmost respect to the WM, when taking the Candidate by the RH and the correct PG the command given is, 'Rise *duly* obligated MMM' and NOT '*newly*'.

When giving instructions for the Candidate to proceed to the Quarries and re-enter the Lodge under the guidance of the SD, the WM will find it useful if he gives a little extra emphasis to the words, 'as a *Mark Man*'.

The preparations for the Deacons and the Candidate to re-enter the Lodge can vary with established traditions. For example, there are Lodges who insist that 'the three workmen' should remove their jackets and roll up their sleeves. But in the main most Lodges will follow faithfully the well-written and detailed instructions given in the 'blue book'. Both Deacons should make a point of studying and being fully conversant with the preparation instructions and not depend wholly on the Tyler who may be, as he is in some Lodges, a relatively inexperienced officer. Preparations are often also supervised by the D of C or his assistant.

It is also important at this stage to be mindful that the Lodge is to all intents and purposes working in the second Degree and will continue as such until the Candidate is entrusted with the Secrets of the MMM's Degree.

It is at this stage of the Ceremony that the Overseers become the focus of much attention. The examination of the materials for the building of the Holy Temple by the Overseers ought to be among the most important and best enacted features of the ceremony. Unfortunately our Overseers are badly prepared. And this is true of far too many Mark Lodges. The 'blue books' lie conspicuously on their Pedestals. Two of the books incidentally are out of date and only the third has been amended in accordance with the revised ritual dated 1992. So the stones are neither going to be examined nor handled correctly. The up-to-date ritual describes accurately and in meticulous detail the words and actions of each of the Overseers. Each individual Overseer's contribution is an essential part of a team effort to determine the suitability and quality of the Stones for the building. Each Overseer has his plans and instructions before him denoting the exact requirements. He should therefore be authoritative, look each workman in the eye and give his verdict in his normal speaking voice. For some strange reason the Candidate is usually spoken to in a singsong voice when referring to his curiously wrought Stone. It is therefore worth repeating this suggestion. Look each workman in the eye and communicate your judgement in your usual tone of voice. As mentioned previously in the earlier section describing the duties of the Overseers, there is more to the role than a hasty glance would indicate.

The Master Overseer calls a council of his Brother Overseers. The Master is much better prepared than both his Junior or his Senior Overseer. The Junior and Senior Overseers present themselves, each taking with him as a lifeline the 'blue book'. The result is a gawky and somewhat ungainly spectacle. Each Overseer, when offering his explanation to the Master, has to hold the KS in front of him with both hands. Neither has prepared his dialogue well enough. So each in turn attempts to partly read it from the book. The rest is left to the imagination.

The KS is rejected and ordered to be heaved among the rubbish. Follow the ritual to the letter at this stage. Don't try to hide the KS. In any event imagine yourself the Craftsman who has spent time, energy and much expertise sculpturing the KS. When the Stone is taken from him to be heaved over, he is going to follow carefully every movement of its whereabouts. In due course and later in the Ceremony it will be much more natural and credible for him instinctively to take the initiative and move directly to where he knows the Stone to be 'hidden'. This is preferable to the comedy of the Deacons play-acting a search.

The shuffling of feet to indicate the impatience of the Craftsmen is purely symbolic in this Lodge. It is not overdone and ceases immediately the SW gavels and rises with FC Sign. The Craftsmen are assembled and the JW moves directly to the North side of the SW's Pedestal to discharge his special duty. The Mark Master's Chant is sung. The column which is led by the JD moves off as they begin the last verse. Members of the Lodge all stand during the Chant and sit when it is completed. The Candidate at the end of the Column is guided by the SD. It is traditional in this particular Lodge for the SD to block off bodily the Wicket surrounded by the square so that the Candidate has no alternative but to present his hand at the Wicket surrounded by the triangle. The reason argued is that it could be considered unfair and deceptive for the SD to mislead, on purpose, the Candidate by indicating the wrong Wicket.

What follows should be a battle of words rather than an affray or struggle. Nevertheless the JD should keep a firm grasp of the shaft of the JW's A-E whilst vouching for the Candidate as an MM. It is hoped also that the JW himself will not be too physical and allow the SD to speak his words clearly and with passion. Experience indicates that when there is too much of a commotion the exchange of words becomes garbled and unintelligible.

The SW states, 'On these conditions I release him.'

Worthy of mention at this particular stage in the ritual are a few small subtleties which for the most part are ignored in most ceremonies, and which should be kept in mind for the sake of the perfection we seek to achieve in the Mark Degree. The first one is the position of the JW's A-E head when he proceeds to discharge his special duty. The head then changes position and points downwards after the SW releases the Candidate and the SD relaxes his grip on the shaft. The next is the keen sense of urgency with which the SD conducts the Candidate directly to the WM. The ritual states 'quick pace'. And of course the SD should be just that little bit out of breath. Finally the Brethren are told to be seated but not until *after* the JW resumes his station, is seated, and the A-E is placed on his Pedestal.

Both the enactments at the SW's Pedestal and the earlier work of the Overseers' examination of the materials will give a pretty good indication whether or not the Officers really know their ritual. And of course there is much more to come. Now it is the WM who is the focus of attention. The manner in which he admonishes the Candidate will only be dramatic and memorable provided he really knows and lives his words. It will be remembered that when discussing the WM's duties, it was recommended that he should begin serious study on reaching the Warden's Chair. One can now visualise more easily the dangers of hurried and last minute learning.

There is *no shuffling* to draw attention to the work at a standstill. Silence is the best indication of all. The KS is missing! The WM who remembers issuing the design for the KS calls for an explanation from his Overseers; each Overseer individually, commencing with the Junior. Once again the Overseers appear to be at loggerheads with the ritual. We seldom see them follow the instructions how to leave their Pedestals, approach the WM, take the step and salute as an FC, accept and examine the plan, pass on the information, step, salute and each return to his Pedestal in the recommended manner. One can only guess that the cause is, as previously stated, hurried or panic reading and last minute learning.

And so, in this manner, the Officers of our fictitious Lodge continue to guide us in what to look out for in this 'Written Rehearsal'. And in the steps we have to take to ensure that this beautiful, edifying and enlightening ritual and exegesis teaches us, in the final instance, how to mark well.

The search for the KS provides no problem. As mentioned earlier, our Craftsman knows exactly where his masterpiece has been heaved over and cast aside amongst the rubble. He moves directly towards it, followed by both Deacons. The SD who has done an impeccable job all through the Ceremony and continues to do so, ever mindful of all the correct procedures, takes his proper stance and informs the WM in a clear audible voice that the KS is found.

The WM checks that the ks conforms exactly with his plan and is ready to entrust the Craftsman with the Secrets of the MMM's Degree.

This important part of the ritual is considered by most MMMs to be the climax of the whole Ceremony. Yet it is only a few years ago since most WMs were happy to delegate this part of the Ceremony to an experienced Past Master. Even he was probably wanting in his knowledge. These were the days when few gave the SIGN M correctly, if at all. And no one knew for sure the ancient word. Some interpretations of this word were quite beyond belief. Yet many were happy to pass them on as being authentic.

This has all been put right within the last ten years since our ritual became more informative and helpful. Especially with the Signs.

There are several reasons why wrong information was passed from one to another. One main reason which concerns us at this particular moment is that demonstrations were hidden in a small corner of the Lodge away from the view of most members, instead of being seen clearly by as many members of the Lodge as possible. This happens even today. To move the Candidate directly to the North side of the WM's pedestal is to obscure him from the clear vision of too many of the Brethren. In addition, both he and the SD inevitably keep tripping over the feet of the seated Grand Officers and other dignitaries, should they be present. In an old Mark Ritual book dated 1926 there is written an 'inked in' amendment. 'Place Candidate in front of WM's Pedestal *not* at North side.' The signs demonstrated by the WM from his Chair, with the Candidate suitably placed in front of the Pedestal, can be seen and enjoyed by all.

Alternatively the Candidate can be placed level to the North end of the WM's Pedestal but a good two paces West, with both Candidate and SD facing South. In which case the WM leaves his Chair and at a suitable distance faces the Candidate. From this position the Signs can be clearly demonstrated, a pleasure for all to see. The Candidate has space and finds it easier to copy correctly. The SD can see what is happening and assist the Candidate if required. When demonstrating the Signs in this manner the WM, from the floor of the Lodge, should always be close enough to his Pedestal to interpose with his gavel when required. There is no need to dwell here on the actual demonstration of the Signs except to say that it should not be rushed. One more example of 'making haste slowly'. Do not allow the Candidate to get away with a wrongly made Sign. Ask him to repeat the ancient word at least twice to get the pronunciation correct. The habit of seeing the Signs given correctly is salutary and of much benefit to future Masters.

The demonstration of the Signs is interpolated by the Chaplain's readings from the Scriptures. Surely, as suggested earlier, it projects a much more reverential and pious image if the Chaplain reads from his own personal VSL, (preferably Masonic version), rather than from his 'blue book'. We should also keep in mind constantly the overall effect of the complete Ceremony on the Candidate. This can best be brought about by the example of confidence displayed and by the sincerity of our actions and general behaviour. As well as enjoying the experience, the newly advanced Brother should become very much aware of the moral advantages of the rank of MMM.

The newly advanced Brother is now conducted to the West and to the SW who in turn presents him to the WM for some mark of his approval. Make note at this stage the SW gives the SIGN M and stands to order with the H SIGN. The WM delegates the SW to invest the newly advanced Brother with the badge and jewel of a Mark Master Mason. The Deacons now remove their Working Aprons and put on their collars. The mechanics of doing this often vary from one Lodge to another. The important thing, however, is to ensure that the newly advanced Brother is not left unattended. The SW now invests him with the badge and jewel of an MMM. It is good practice to make sure beforehand that the new Brother's Apron has been adjusted to his waist size.

The WM now adds to the observations made by the SW. When discussing the jewel, the SD should remove his own jewel and use it as a model to illustrate the comments of the WM. For example, the English letters HTWS STKS which are synonyms of the Hebrew characters on the obverse. These Hebrew characters are pronounced *Hé kaph aleph shin lamed shin Mem Yod* meaning *Khiram ben almonah shálakh l' Sheló-moh mólek Israel.* And the translation is exactly the same as the English letters, *Hiram the widow's son sent to King Solomon.* [see photograph page 58]. As a matter of general interest, both the English and Hebrew versions are contained in the ritual as practised by the King Solomon's Quarries Lodge No. 828 which now meets at Mark Masons' Hall. The King Solomon's Quarries Lodge was consecrated in Jerusalem in the Underground Quarries where they held their meetings until 1948 when they were obliged to re-form in London following the troubles and general unrest in the Holy Land at that time. The WM's Address on the badge and jewel should end with some emphasis on the importance of the Brother using his Mark after his signature whenever in correspondence with a Brother MMM, and when signing the Lodge register.

The presentation of the Working Tools is always an opportunity to contribute to the development of a junior member of the Lodge, allowing him to participate in the Ceremony. He should be given due praise for work well done. Both the WM and the D of C should congratulate him personally. He should not be allowed to have an unsuccessful experience. Should things go wrong, which they do sometimes, even among the best of us, then it is for the WM and the D of C to bolster up his self assurance, and allay his disappointment and fears by talking to him of their own similar experiences. Then they should remind him of those parts of his delivery which he did very well, in particular… Otherwise our junior member may never wish to participate again. And so the Ceremony of Advancement comes to an end with the WM's final recitation to the newly Advanced Brother in which he summarises the sublime precepts of this delightful and honourable Degree. It is a beautiful Address and it should be the climax or culmination of the WM's dedicated preparation and industry over a fairly long period of time. There is no satisfaction like that of a goal realised, a worthwhile achievement. The final precept offered in this gratifying dissertation is that contained in Psalm 118, Vs 22, 'The stone which the builders refused is become the head stone of the corner.' The Hebrew version which is likewise part of the ritual of King Solomon's Quarries Lodge and which is also inscribed in Hebrew characters on our Tracing Board is, *Eben mé-asu habonim hay-thah l'rosh pinnah'* [see photograph page 59].

The WM invites the newly advanced Brother to take his seat in a Mark Master Masons' Lodge. He welcomes him warmly and offers his sincere congratulations. The SD escorts him to his seat in the south-east. He also congratulates him and reminds him that he has been an ideal Candidate. Another job well done.

חִירָם בֶּן־אַלְמֹנָה שָׁלַח לִ שְׁלֹמֹה מֶלֶךְ יִשְׂרָאֵל
L A R S I　　K L M　　H M L SH　　L　　KH L SH　　H N M L A　　N B　　M R I KH

= Khiram ben almónah shárlakh l' sheló-moh mélek Israel.
= Hiram son of (the) widow sent to Solomon king of Israel.

English - חבא שלש מי = חָבָא שָׁלֹשׁ מִי = Khárba shálésh me.
= He hid three (things) from me.

Scottish - חירס בן אלמנה איש צור שלח מלך שלמה = חבא אאצצ שמש
H M L SH　　K L M　　KH L SH　　R O T Z　　SH I A　　H N M L A　　N B　　M R I KH

= Hiram son of (the) widow, a man of Tyre, sent (to) King Solomon.

חֲבֵרִי־אוֹת = Khabáy-ree Oath (spelt "Khabérii Aoth")
TH　　O A　　I R E KH

= Companions of the mark.

שַׂר־הַבּוֹנִים = Sár hab-bónim = Chief of the builders.
M I N O B B H　　R S

Copy of old document papers
Copy of old document papers from King Solomon's Quarries Lodge of Mark Master Masons No. 828 Jerusalem.

CLOSING THE LODGE

All Lodge business on the Summons having been completed, the WM alone stands for the Risings. First, Second, Third and Fourth.

Immediately following the Third and Fourth Rising, the SD collects the Working Plans and places them on the SW's Pedestal. Exactly as detailed in the ritual. The reason it is mentioned here at all, is that this simple part of the Closing Ceremony is often forgotten and leads to panic corrective action by the SD when the SW is asked if the Working Plans have been so deposited.

It is fortunate that the Chaplain is able to recite the closing prayer by heart and does not have to produce the unwanted 'blue book'. If, however, the Chaplain has decided to use his own personal copy of the VSL, reading the prayers from notes inserted in the VSL would be quite acceptable.

On Mark Tracing Board are the words from Psalm cxviij. 22 —

אֶבֶן מָאֲסוּ הַבּוֹנִים הָיְתָה לְרֹאשׁ פִּנָּה

H NNP   SH   A   RL   H   THi H   MI N OBB H   US AM NB A

Eben máh-asu hab-bó-nim hay-thah l'rosh pinnah.

Eben = a stone
máh-asu = they rejected
hab-bónim = the builders
hay-thah = is (become)
l'rosh = for a head of
pinnah = a corner.

Old document papers
Copy of old document papers from King Solomon's Quarries Lodge of Mark Master Masons No. 828 Jerusalem.

The WM should remember that he gavels with the *left* hand. Then it is the SW who closes the Lodge by command of the WM. The SW should be aware that he is now the pacemaker concerning the third part of the first Sign. And the Lodge members should await his guidance. The JD should remember to proceed without his Wand and to adjust the Tracing Board. The IPM goes to the front of the WM's Pedestal, short court bow, removes the M AND C, closes the VSL, salutes, and returns to his station to announce the last remaining words according to ancient custom.

APPENDIX TO THE WRITTEN REHEARSAL

The reader is reminded again that the 'Written Rehearsal' is an invented narrative. However, the fact that it is based on an attentive appraisal of a goodly number of Mark Ceremonies over a period of some thirty-five years by an enthusiastic Mark Mason may lend to it an air of authenticity and, we hope, authority. The examples referred to do not concern any one Lodge, or any specific group of Lodges. Neither do they focus on any one particular geographical region.

The Mark Degree has still to be discovered by many Craft Masons. The general information contained in this book, and those refinements of ritual practice gleaned from the 'Written Rehearsal' will serve to dramatise and project the enticing image of Mark Masonry. There is no better publicity among members of the Fraternity than to hear them talk about the pleasures of belonging to a particular Degree. Help them to discover how to mark well.

'To each is given a bag of tools
A shapeless mass and a book of rules,
And each must make e'er time is flown,
A stumbling block, or a stepping stone'
Anon 18th century

Lectures

At the end of the Ceremony of Advancement, the WM tells the newly advanced Brother that on some future occasion his attention will be directed to a 'lecture expounding the history of the Degree and explaining the origins of our ceremony and signs'. Included, of course, is the Lecture on the Tracing Board of the Degree of Mark Master Mason. Sadly we seldom hear these lectures in Lodge even though both are enlightening and instructive, containing a wealth of information about the Degree. The main reason given for neglecting this important part of our ritual is the actual Advancement Ceremony itself which, in addition to taking precedence, takes up much time and is likely to tax the capabilities of the Officers who already have plenty of work to do.

There is a possible answer. *The Catechetical Lecture.* A bit of a mouthful to say perhaps. It simply means oral communication or instruction by question and answer. If we examine the number of members in Lodge. including certain Officers, then we have two Wardens who are not overworked. There are also Past Masters of the Lodge who would like to be involved. Let us say two Stewards whose participation would be an important part of their Masonic development. And equally important the Lodge Secretary, the Treasurer, the Registrar of Marks, and last but not by any means least, the Organist. There is an excellent opportunity for these Officers and members of the Lodge who would not normally have the occasion to take part in the Advancememt Ceremony and who would welcome the opportunity to participate in the Lectures. The Lecture on the Tracing Board, for example, is conveniently divided into meaningful sections under various headings. Members of the Lodge participating are allocated one, perhaps two, sections. This makes for light work and no one member of the Lodge is overburdened with too much to do. These details must be carefully planned and participants given adequate notice. It is a good idea for the Lectures to be included in the WM's general plan for the year, and the participants to be named.

The WM himself may care to begin the Lecture by leading with the symbolic significance of the VSL. When finished he calls upon Brother 'x' to give the symbolic explanation of the 'All-Seeing Eye' and the 'Chisel' and so forth. It is suggested that the final section 'The Equilateral Triangle' is promoted to a distinctive status to be delivered by one or perhaps two specially selected Past Masters as a mark of prestige or honour.

The Lecture on the Mark Master Masons' Degree does not lend itself as easily to the catechetical procedure as that of the Tracing Board. It works, however, if divided, once again, into meaningful paragraphs and allocated to the participating Brethren. The WM controls, calling each Brother by name. On completion of his piece the Brother gives a short court bow, and the WM calls on the next Brother to continue, and so on.

If it is estimated that the complete Lecture cannot be given at any single meeting because of the time factor, then deliver half the Lecture. This way, we won't ignore the Lectures as we may have done in the past. The Target should be both Lectures to be given in a Master's year.

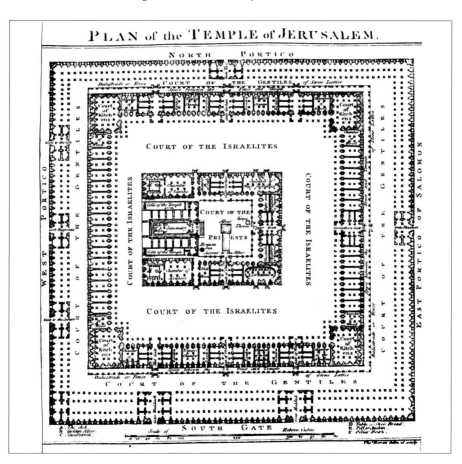

Materials for the Building of King Solomon's Temple

When we remind ourselves that it was the choosing of a Mark by each and every Operative Fellowcraft Mason which made possible the organisation and administration of the building of King Solomon's Temple, then we cannot help but feel a sense of pride and importance to be a Mark Master Mason and to belong to this ancient, amicable and reverential Degree. We can repay this privilege by setting a good example both in Temple and elsewhere among members of other Degrees. A visionary concept of the materials for the building of the Temple, the workmen employed, evidence of Masons' marks, and rejected Stones, can only serve to improve the enactment of our ritual in Temple, and give Mark Masons the reserve power of knowledge to talk about the lore of the Mark Degree to other members of the Fraternity.

The Lecture on the Mark Master Masons' Degree describes 80,000 Operatives employed, plus a levy of 30,000 in the forests of Lebanon. There were probably many more than that as is implied in the Old Testament. 1 Kings, Chapter 5, Vs 15 and 16 make mention of an extra 70,000, 'that bare burdens'. Admittedly such bearers of burdens would not be craftsmen. But were they Entered Apprentices? Also in 2 Chronicles, Chapter 2, Vs 18, the number of Overseers given is 3600, that is 300 more than is contained in our Mark Lecture. In a paper entitled the Finch Lectures (1802), the writer maintained that the extra 300 Overseers were in fact the 'Principal Rulers over the whole'.

This seems to make good sense. In all, the figures show that some 153,000 workmen were involved. If we subtract the 70,000 bearers of burdens, then it brings us back to 80,000 Operatives plus the Overseers. The extra 300 Overseers 'over the whole' due to their seniority were probably not considered part of the workforce.

The actual size of the Temple itself is given in 1 Kings, Chapter 6, Vs 2. Length 60 cubits, breadth 20 cubits and the height 30 cubits. If we agree on the cubit as being about 20 inches then the dimensions were 100 x 35 x 50 feet. The Porchway or Entrance was 18 feet deep and both pillars were approximately 65 feet high including the chapiters. Not exactly a massive building. The whole Temple site, however, covered an area of some 35 acres

Left: **Plan of the Temple Chapter at Jerusalem**
The Sanctum Sanctorum, The Ark of the Covenant, The Pillars Boaz and Jachin

on which were constructed many important and impressive buildings, including King Solomon's Palace, the Queen's Palace, the Court of Justice, and the House of the Cedars of Lebanon.

When it is written that Jerusalem was built on four hills, the hills referred to are Mount Zion, Mount Moriah, Mount Akra and Mount Bezetha. When seven hills are mentioned then Mount Scopus, the Mount of Olives and the Mount of Offence are also included. The Temple area of Jerusalem was built on Mount Moriah, which in its natural state was a narrow ridge of rock known as the Hog's Back. It was a honeycomb of caves branched and widely intersected by gullies and still more caves. At the top of Mount Moriah was the threshing floor of Arauna the Jebusite. David King of Israel bought this threshing floor, built an altar and later commanded his son Solomon to build on the site a Temple to the Lord. The task of Hiram and his builders was an enormous one, to convert this small hill into a vast platform, 1500 feet by 1,000 feet, and filled with stone up to a height of 150 feet. The centre was the original Mount Moriah and the building of the foundations when finished was not completely filled in. Many large vaults and subterranean chambers were left as granaries and water cisterns. These still exist. There is the story that when Hiram viewed the site he disagreed with Solomon and suggested, as an alternative, the hill Bezetha or Mount Scopus, both being higher, of greater width, and requiring less construction. This is probably pure conjecture since one imagines that King David had sound reasons for choosing Mount Moriah, already of historical significance since this was the place where Abraham was told to go in order to sacrifice his son Isaac.

A lot of stone would be required for the foundations and later for the Temple and the other majestic and imposing buildings yet to be built on the site. Worshipful Brother 'Daddy' Cowell who was for many years Secretary of the King Solomon's Quarries Lodge No. 828, Jerusalem, which now meets at Mark Masons' Hall, London, made copious notes when the Lodge met in the Underground Quarries in Jerusalem. He wrote:

'Palestine abounds in stone and all over the Holy Land are wonderful examples of the stone masons' art. But much nearer at hand are the vast underground quarries of King Solomon which lie beneath ancient Jerusalem. There is no doubt as to the antiquity of them. Pottery and carvings, notably of the man-faced winged beast, (bull or lion), of Assyria, help to decide this, [see photograph page 65], *and in*

recent years we have established the fact that the stones of the lowest and oldest courses of the walls of the Temple Area are similar in composition to the stone in the underground Quarries and even fit the vacant places.'

Assyrian stone carving, Man-faced Winged Beast Bull or Lion
Discovered in the Royal Quarries of King Solomon underneath the City of Jerusalem. This stone and other pieces of pottery and carvings indicate the great antiquity of the Quarries which produced the Stone for the building of the Temple.

The great wall which surrounds the Temple area has very ancient and deep foundations, seventy feet of it are above the ground, and eighty feet below the surface. In 1871, the celebrated archaeologist Sir Charles Warren sank a deep shaft at the southeast corner of the wall and at the bottom found extremely well-dressed stones bearing marks. 'Masons' Marks' he called them. They were in the form of letters and figures in red paint. The characters were considered to be Phoenician. They were in an excellent state of preservation after 3000 years by reason of being covered with soil. General Sir Charles Warren, a founder member and first President of the Quatuor Coronati Lodge of Masonic Research, describes them as being 'the marks of King Solomon'.

The stone from the Quarries is a crystalline limestone and, when dressed, frequently reveals traces of sea-shells and fossils. The theory is that at the time of the Great Flood, Jerusalem was an island, surrounded by the waters which inundated the stone in the quarries beneath the City. Hence the sea-shells and fossils embedded in them. The stone takes an excellent polish and buildings made from it have a sparkle that can be seen from a far distance. This may have inspired Flavius Josephus, the eminent Jewish historian, to describe King Solomon's Temple as 'glistening in the sun like a mound of snow'.

The methods of hewing the stone are the subject of many legends. The use of metal was not permitted anywhere near the vicinity of the Temple. 'And the house, when it was in building, was built of stone made ready before it was brought thither — so that there was neither hammer nor axe nor any tool of iron heard in the house, while it was in building.' (1 Kings, Chapter 6, Vs 7)

In the Quarries there are indications of grooves made in the stone in which wooden wedges were placed. Water was then poured on the wedges causing expansion or swelling which broke or split the stone. The Jewish Talmud and Mishna say that the stone for the Temple was not cut with metal tools but with the Shamir, translated in the Bible as Adamant, an extremely hard stone like flint or diamond. Other references in the writings of the Rabbis say that the 'Shamir' was a seed of barley which when placed in a crevice in the stone, grew, swelled, and finally split the rock. A further Jewish reference source, the Tosefta Treatise, Sota 9.6. states that Solomon used a worm (spiral screw) called Shamir to cut through the stone. There are many legends concerning the cutting of the stone and great emphasis made on the exclusion of metal from the Temple area. 'For if thou lift up any tool or iron upon it, thou hast polluted it.' Exodus, Chapter 20, Vs 25. The stone was a crystalline limestone called Maklaki and found only in the 'Royal Quarries'. Specially dressed and polished, the stone was used as a facing for the Temple from the foundation to the coping. It was also called 'Mezzeh' by the Arab Masons, and has the quality of hardening on exposure to the air. Such stones smoothed and squared, polished and marked by skilful craftsman and watchful overseers were hauled down the Tyropoenian valley, and from there hoisted up to their proper place in the intended structure.

There are still many caverns in existence today with the remains of early workings or tasks: half hewn blocks, niches for earthenware lamps, hewn water cisterns and lots of crude pottery.

In one such cavern, the King Solomon's Quarries Lodge of Mark Master Masons No. 828 was consecrated in the year 1926. And the Lodge met

King Solomon's Quarries

Right: The entrance to King Solomon's Quarries from a distance.

Below: A close-up of the entrance to King Solomon's Quarries.

regularly there until they were forced to leave Palestine in 1948 because of the great unrest in the country at that time. The height of the cavern was fifteen feet and it had a floor of stone chippings some thirty feet deep, a reminder of the labour of countless Mark Master Craftsmen in those ancient days. Special working aprons were worn and sandbags used as kneeling stools. The Master and Wardens made themselves comfortable seated on large stone blocks, and other members of the Lodge including the Overseers sat on chairs carried down into the cavern Temple by prisoners from the local gaol. Under escort, of course. The Master, Senior and Junior Overseers were seated at the right hand of the Worshipful Master, Senior and Junior Wardens respectively — the only Lodge in the English Constitution to have the permission of Grand Lodge to do so. The Pedestals used were large blocks of stone. Walking on stone chippings is not easy. One tends to slide, lose balance and even stagger, making it a bit difficult to 'process in' with a modicum of dignity. Processions in and out of the Temple were thus dispensed with, even when receiving and welcoming Grand Officers and other high ranking dignitaries. Over the years this deficiency has become a tradition of the Lodge which is still practised to this day.

The excerpt which now follows is a translation from the Hebrew. An extract from Volume 2 of 'Nach Jerusalem', by Dr Ludwig August Frankl, Vienna, 1860, and should interest every Mark Master Mason.

'When we cast our eyes on the walls of the city to our right, we saw in passing the Zion Gate, and the deep valley of Beth Hinnom to our left. Opposite the wall of the city, where is the site of the Temple, are scattered here and there, large and wide stones without limit, twenty-two feet in length, — which have been there without doubt, as eloquent proclaimers of the desolation of time, which destroys all incidents, — in the original position that the craftsmen left them thousands of years ago.

They also indicated to us, in the same place a block of stone, seven feet and a half in thickness, which the builders of Solomon's Temple rejected because it was not sufficiently beautiful to be received into the building, and so they cast it away. But is this the only stone that withstood the Shamir, which was placed according to tradition on every stone to split it into two parts, as iron was not to be raised upon the Temple, the Tabernacle of Peace?'

The materials mentioned most frequently in the Bible are, of course, Stone and Cedar wood. Quoting from the 2nd Book of Chronicles, Chapter 2, Vs 3

King Solomon's Quarries

The vast Chambers inside the Quarry

and 4: 'And Solomon sent to Hiram, King of Tyre, saying, As thou didst deal with David my father and didst send him Cedars to build him an house to dwell therein, even so deal with me. Behold, I build an house to the name of the Lord my God.' Then Vs 11 and 16: 'And Hiram King of Tyre answered in writing, which he sent to Solomon... and we shall cut wood out of Lebanon, as much as thou shalt need: and we will bring it to thee in floats by sea to Joppa; and thou shalt carry it up to Jerusalem.' The Lebanon of the old testament was famous for its mountain range and its forests. Mention is also made of the 'Snows of Lebanon' and of the country's fertility. But it is famous most of all for its great Cedar trees. Ezekiel describes them as 'the glory of Lebanon'. The majesty of the groves is most impressive and one is led to believe from the many Biblical allusions that the Cedar is indeed the king of trees. The Cedar is described again as 'a noble tree, the glory of the vegetable kingdom of Palestine, and so is made the symbol of grandeur, might, loftiness and of wide expansion'. It grows rapidly and lives to a great age [see photograph page 71]. Bsherrah, where the groves are situated, is 6,000 feet above sea level. The roads are sharply graded and a guide book of the area states that on the road to the coast there are 118 hairpin bends. There is a copious supply of water and it is certain that the enormous trunks were conveyed down in water chutes similar to the ones used in Norway today. It is not known for certain to which port the timber was taken before being conveyed on floats by sea to Joppa [see photograph page 71]. Tripoli is the nearest port but is not referred to until around 700BC. On the other hand, Tyre was known 2,000 years earlier and was a big and flourishing port at the time of Hiram, besides being his home town. It seems, therefore, the likeliest port of embarkation. The great river Leontes, or Lîtânî, which rises near Baalbek, runs into the sea five miles north of Tyre. In summer it is but a gentle, flowing stream up in the mountains. As the snows of the Lebanon melt, it becomes a torrent.

If we take a look at the map of Palestine, preferably a map of Biblical times, (see Holy Bible, Masonic Edition, Maps 1, the Kingdoms of Judah and Israel, and 2, The Dominions of David and Solomon), we can accompany the floats as they pass down the coast to Joppa. Beginning at Bsherrah then to Tripoli, Jebail, Beirut, Sidon, Tyre, Acre, Haifa and Joppa. Joppa with its steep shores was, and still is, reputedly a bad harbour where ships unload passengers and freight with great difficulty. Little appears to have been written about the final stage of conveying the timber from Joppa to Jerusalem over the forty-mile steep ascent through the valley of Ajalon. The Rev F W Farrar, author of *Solomon his Life and Times* states that the 'timber was dragged with infinite toil

'Hew me Cedars out of Lebanon'
…said Solomon to Hiram, King of Tyre —

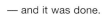

— and it was done.

Joppa — the Rocks in a Storm
'…Masonic tradition informs us that the shore was so steep that it was impossible to ascend from the rafts without assistance from above.

71

up the steep and rocky roads to Jerusalem'. A more plausible account is that of Adam Clarke in his *The Holy Bible with Commentary*, who suggests, 'Hiram could transport the timbers all squared, and not only cut to scantling, but cut, so as to occupy the place intended for it in the building, without further need for axe or saw. The materials had only to be put together when they arrived at Jerusalem.' The amount of timber required for the Temple, and the other majestic buildings on the site of the Temple area, defies calculation. The payment was by annual instalments. 20,000 measures of beaten wheat, 20,000 measures of barley, 20,000 bäths of wine and 20,000 bäths of oil. (2 Chronicles, Chapter 2, Vs 10.) In other words, 160,000 bushels of wheat, 160,000 bushels of barley, 15,000 gallons of oil and 15,000 gallons of wine.

In the clay ground between Succoth and Zeredatha, Hiram Abif cast all the sacred vessels of the Temple. There were altars, basons, lavers, pots, candlesticks, censers, lamps and many, many more including the two Great Pillars. The site of the Temple was 2,600 feet high on the top of Mount Moriah. Succoth, in the plain of Jordan, was some forty-five miles away and 1,200 feet below sea level.

Why then should the wise Solomon go such a distance and to such a trackless area to cast his vessels? The fact that he did have his sacred vessels cast there is confirmed in 1 Kings, Chapter 7, Vs 46 and again 2 Chronicles, Chapter 4, Vs 17. At Succoth or Seikoot there is a special clay of great tenacity, peculiarly fitted for making moulds. This was the clay ground for Hiram's foundries. It was the best matrix clay within reach of Hiram Abif, found only in 'the clay ground between Succoth and Zeredatha', about two days' journey northeast of Jerusalem. The distance was far and most inconvenient, as was the locality, and the journey was equally arduous. But so important was it to Hiram to secure a sharp and perfect mould for his castings that, as the Bible informs us, he established his furnaces there. Hence the great beauty and craftsmanship of the sacred vessels for the Temple. Many were cast in pure gold, and other treasures in 'brass' as well as daily utensils. Much mention is made of 'brass' both in the Old Testament and the Talmud. This is not the commercial brass as we know it. Brass was not known to the Jews in Solomon's time. The biblical word 'brass' stands for bronze. That is, nearly pure copper with an alloy of tin. Bronze is very hard and one of the oldest known metals. King David brought away much bronze from Hermon, but having no craftsman skilled in the metal, he had to send for Hiram Abif, the 'cunning man', or skilled man.

The Temple of King Solomon took seven years to build and was completed in the year 957BC.

Jerusalem
— The Unbroken Link

Undoubtedly the building of Solomon's Temple at Jerusalem gave origin to the tradition of Masonry as we now know it. Therefore we do not wish specially to get involved with masonry or building earlier than this period. However, the Pyramids built in the period 3000 to 2000BC cannot be ignored entirely since they emphasise the importance of the Operative Masons' skills and art. Especially as they are much in evidence to this day — stately, magnificent, resplendent, and a lasting monument to an art which in all ages has been largely devoted to religious purposes. King Solomon's Temple stood for some 371 years until it was finally destroyed by Nebuchadnezzar. Josephus tells us that Jerusalem fell on the ninth day of the fourth month, 586BC, when the City and Solomon's Temple were cast to the flames. The prophet Jeremiah took careful note of the manner of the destruction, how the pillars were pulled down, broken into pieces and conveyed to Babylon on camels. The Temple was utterly destroyed by fire.

As we know, the captivity of the Jews in Babylon lasted seventy years until Cyrus the King of Persia released them in the year 538BC that they might return to Jerusalem and rebuild the City and their Temple. Of the 200,000 released, 50,000 accompanied their Prince Zerubbabel to build a new Temple to be called Zerubbabel's Temple. The remainder of some 150,000 dispersed in many directions, possibly through Armenia to Constantinople, Berea, Thessalonica, Corinth and Athens. And wherever they settled they would build their homes and their Synagogues.

The Babylon of 4,000 years ago was much maligned. Now we know the truth that it was a City of mighty people and a centre of learning. Scientists and archaeologists have dug deeply into the mounds of Mesopotamia to discover its literature and history, preserved to us, written on clay and baked in stone.

Babylonians knew all about square roots, cube roots and fractions, horizontals, levels, and squares. The City itself was built in the form of a square as were the buildings and other local amenities. The quality of life of the Jewish exiles was not one of extreme misery. It is true that some were put to forced labour but most were allowed to settle into communities and build homes and gardens. Some even graduated into high official positions and became potent factors in the national development. In short, much of the culture of the Jews was derived from Babylon. They were encouraged to make use of the numerous large libraries readily available to them. The Jews developed many additional skills in architecture and building during their long captivity and the operative masons were always in demand. Some followed their Prince Zerubbabel back to Jerusalem to build the new Temple. The majority became itinerant and took their skills to neighbouring far off lands.

When Zerubbabel's Temple was in turn despoiled and desecrated by Herod the Great many more skilled masons left Jerusalem and dispersed to foreign parts. Herod's Temple, often referred to as the third Temple, and the Temple which existed in the days of Jesus Christ, was also destroyed, this time by the Romans under Titus in AD70. The Romans had by this time built up a vast Mediterranean Empire and it was destined that Operative Masons and their Apprentices should follow the Roman Legions. They made plans and layouts and built entrenched Roman camps. They constructed bridges and aqueducts and supervised the soldiers and labourers in the erection of these works as well as in the making of roads. In Imperial Rome it was by then the established custom to form all the crafts into unions or colleges. This practice was followed in the vanquished countries of Mediaeval Europe and was in turn introduced into the British Isles by the invading Romans. These colleges were later named Guilds and the place of their meetings was called a Loge or Lodge.

In the year AD43, Emperor Claudius Caesar sent a number of masons to Britain where they built walled camps and other fortifications for protection of the Roman army against the Picts and the Scots. As these Romans settled in Britain their living conditions were made much easier and more comfortable with the construction of baths, villas, temples and bridges. One of the first Roman cities in Britain was at York, then called Eboracum.

Back in Rome the Collegia or Guilds held regular meetings in secluded buildings, specially built for that purpose. They had peculiar Ceremonies and took an oath to help each other and to help any member in distress. There was a Master, Wardens, Fellowcrafts and Apprentices, a Keeper of Archives, Treasurer and Serving Brethren. No mention is made of Deacons. Around this time, AD200, the name 'Brother' came into use among the early Christian fraternity of Masons.

Vesuvius erupted in AD79 and buried Pompeii deep in volcanic lava and ashes. Nearly two thousand years later in 1878 during excavations an ancient

Lodge room was unearthed. The floor was of black and white chequered marble. On one side of the room was a recess with an altar. And on either side of the recess were two Great Pillars. In the corner of the same side was a room seen as a robing room. The walls were decorated with squares, levels, compasses and interlaced triangles. Also found were working tools made of rosewood with brass tips. The stone altar, four feet high, is said to be in the National Museum in Naples. The description of this room was vouched for by an unnamed Past Master of a Preston Lodge who visited Pompeii just before the Second World War. The building was identified as a Collegia of Artificers or Masonic Craftsmen. Otherwise not a lot of detail remains of the character of these Collegia or Guilds. Numerous manuscripts, however, of the charges given to Apprentice Masons are extant and preserved today in the British Museum and others. The Halliwell Manuscript and the Cooke Manuscript are the most ancient of the 'Old Charges'.

Masonry declined in Britain when the Romans abandoned the island around AD407. The successors of the Roman Collegia were associations of travelling 'architects' who journeyed from city to city throughout all the countries on the Continent as well as Britain in the period around AD500. The most famous of these associations was believed by many well-informed Brethren to be 'The Great Order of the Commacine Masons' so named because they fled to the Island of Commacina on Lake Como for refuge when the Goths and Vandals overwhelmed Rome in AD470. These were the early days of Christian dispensation. The building art stood at the height of its influence and power. The expertise of the Commacine Free Masons, for they had already begun to use this distinctive name, had spread throughout many continental countries. It is said that they travelled under the authority of the Pope and that their mission was to build churches, palaces and other stately buildings. When Augustine came to convert Britain, they followed him to erect chapels and shrines. The Venerable Bede in AD674 mentions the fact that Commacine Masons were sent from Gaul to erect the Church at Wearmouth, (now called Sunderland). As Mark Master Masons it is of great interest to us to follow this historical chain of development of our ancestral Brethren to the eighth century AD and to compare the usages and customs with those of today. An inscribed stone dated AD712 shows that the Guilds of Commacine Masons were organised with members, or disciples as they were sometimes called, under *one* Grand Master. They called their meeting places Loggia, had Masters, Wardens, Oaths, Grips, Tokens, Passwords, and wore white Aprons and Gloves. The square, level, plumb rule and arch were among their emblems. They lived in huts or lodges temporarily erected near the buildings on which they were employed.

The Dissolution of the Monasteries by Henry VIII in 1539 restrained the activities of operative masons. Their guilds and lodges were in a dire state financially. They were glad to benefit from the established friendships of outside members to help them with their funds. These friends were of high standing in the community and glad to recognise the non-political atmosphere, the good company and hospitality afforded by these 'architects' or masons. They were invited to join and after their Obligation they were called 'Free and Accepted Masons'. Not a lot is known about these early 'Free and Accepted Masons' since nothing was written or printed about Masonry. We do know that these men comprised high ecclesiastics, men of science and wealthy nobles who were anxious to patronise and encourage the art of Operative Masonry. As academics they confined themselves to philosophical speculations concerning the principles of the art and symbolising the moral qualities of its labours, its implements and working tools. And so there was a division of the membership into two classes. The practical and the theoretical, or as we now know them, the Operative and the Speculative. There are also historical details recording the involvement of the nobility as Grand Masters of Operative Masonry from the time of Alfred the Great, William the Conqueror and King John of Magna Carta fame, who in 1199 appointed a Peter de Colechurch as Grand Master, to rebuild London Bridge in stone.

There is little doubt that such knowledge influenced the higher echelons of society to take an interest in the art and as speculative masons to exert greater influence by reason of their higher culture and wealth.

The Great Fire of London in 1666 though disastrous for the City and its citizens was in fact a providential affair which had a far reaching consequence on the future greatness of this country and on Freemasonry as we know it today. At this period in time, operative Lodges were relatively few and limited in numbers. They had a more vigorous existence in the North of England and in Scotland. There were Lodges in Glasgow and Kilwinning, for example, whose traditions had been maintained from the 12th century. Other Lodges in York, Melrose and Aberdeen have records giving us an insight into the unity, order, beliefs and ideals of these early Masons. As every schoolboy knows, in the Great Fire of London, St Paul's Cathedral and practically the whole City was gutted. The gigantic problem of rebuilding had to be faced. The renowned Christopher Wren, who was in Paris at the time and en route for Italy was asked to return to his native shores and take on this herculean challenge. He responded immediately and within days of the Great Fire of London having been extinguished, he had formulated a plan for the rebuilding of London. The plan was not implemented but Wren was made one of the six members of the commission for rebuilding London. He designed St Paul's Cathedral and the first stone was laid in 1675. A vast number of masons were sent for and employed. They came from all parts of the Continent, in addition to a goodly number from Scotland and the North of England. The Cathedral was completed in 1711. Also some 51 churches, among them St Stephen's (Walbrook), St Lawrence Jewry, Christ Church (Newgate Street). St Mary-le-Bow (Cheapside), to name but a few. And many of his 51 churches still stand today, the objects of much pride and wonder. But his masterpiece was St Paul's. He died in 1723, a man fulfilled. The itinerant operative masons, accustomed to their Guilds and Lodges, naturally formed several in London, the first being at the 'Goose and Gridiron' in St Paul's Churchyard. Others included the 'Apple Tree Tavern' in Charles Street, Covent Garden, and the 'Rummer and Grapes Tavern' in Channel Row, Westminster. In those days Lodges just took their names from the Inn or Hostelry where they met.

The need for operative Guilds and Lodges to continue with their building programmes throughout the land indicates that Mark Masonry made great progress through the years up to the time of the Act of Union of the two Grand Lodges in 1813. Article 2 of this Act must have been bewildering at the time to all Mark Masons because it declared that pure ancient Masonry consists of the three Craft Degrees, the Royal Arch and no more. It goes beyond the scope of this book to attempt to analyse why the very substance of Craft Masonry should be so ignored. And one could reasonably argue that the distilled essence of the knowledge of the mason's art from the time of the Pharaohs was ignored likewise. The historical narrative of Mark Masons from the earliest times of King Solomon, Hiram King of Tyre and Hiram Abif, and Adoniram, like the Bible, has had to rely on many sources for its preservation. But it does make a lot of sense. And there is sufficient evidence to prove its feasibility. The Declaration that 'The Mark Masters' Degree did *not* form a part of Royal Arch Masonry, was *not* essential to Craft Masonry' was, to say the least, a most unimaginative statement but it did lead, as described earlier, to Brother Lord Leigh taking the initiative with other distinguished Brethren to form the first Grand Lodge of Mark Master Masons.

The heritage of Operative Masonry and Mark Masonry is colourful and exciting as an art mostly devoted to religious purposes and the creation of beautiful buildings with perfection always in mind. The oath taken in the

Collegia or Guilds in Rome by our ancient Brethren to help each other and to assist any member in distress is still written into our ritual. It is the dominant message conveyed to every new Mark Master Mason when he is congratulated by the Worshipful Master on his Advancement to this honourable Degree in Freemasonry.

The Degree of the Mark Master Mason lives on as a lasting monument to the early craftsmen who began the work of the Great Overseer with the building of King Solomon's Temple and to those who continue to do so, not only in Stone but in the building and the cementing of good human relations and lasting friendships.

There is now no trace of any of the three Temples, but the site of the threshing floor of Arauna the Jebusite on which King Solomon erected the altar and built the first Temple is now known as the Dome of the Rock and has been described as the most exquisite building in Jerusalem. The area came into the possession of the Muslims in AD637 and the Dome of the Rock or Noble Sanctuary, as the Arabs call it, was built in AD1022. This Sacred Site is venerated alike by Muslims, Jews and Christians.

Too many Craft Masons are unaware of the rich history of the Mark Degree and its legendary unsevered link with Jerusalem; and why it has earned the reputation as 'The Friendly Degree'. As Mark Master Masons we can help to make better known this well-deserved reputation, by dedicated attention to our work in the Temple, having a good background knowledge of its history and development, and a friendly eagerness to give permissible replies to genuinely interested questioners.

'A man, Sir, should keep his friendship in constant repair'
Dr Samuel Johnson (1755)

The Dome of the Rock
According to legend, the Sacred or Holy Rock on the top of Mount Moriah was the place where Abraham offered up Isaac, and where Jacob had his vision of the ladder ascending to Heaven. Here also was the site of the threshing floor of Arauna the Jebusite which King David bought and on which he ordered his son Solomon to build a Temple. The Dome of the Rock as it is now was built over the Sacred Rock or Sakhra in AD1022. The site came into possession of the Muslims in AD637, and except for a period of 88 years when it was occupied by Crusaders (1099–1187) it has been in their hands ever since.

Holy rock Moriah from the North

Holy rock Moriah from the South

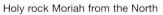

Holy rock Moriah from the Dome

81

Chronology

All Freemasons reading this book will hopefully find a good deal of interest in the following list of some outstanding events in the Development of Freemasonry since the building of King Solomon's Temple to the formation of Mark Grand Lodge. Some of the dates are controversial. However, since they are based on the authoritative writings of such distinguished Masons as R F Gould, L Vibert, R C Davies, D Knoop and D P Jones as well as the Masonic Year Book, they may be assumed to be reasonably correct.

BC

957   King Solomon's Temple completed.

714   Collegia Artificium — the College of Artificers, Roman Gilds, or Corporations of Craftsmen instituted in Rome.

587   King Solomon's Temple destroyed by Nebuzaradan under Nebuchadnezzar. Altogether the sieges of Jerusalem cover a period of twenty years. It has been estimated that the total number of Israelites deported to Babylon was between 500,000 and 1,000,000.

539   Cyrus releases Jews from their captivity. According to Josephus only some 50,000 returned under the leadership of Zerubbabel to Jerusalem to rebuild the Temple. 30,000 of this number were adult men. The remainder were women and children. Many opted to remain in Babylon. It is estimated that 150,000 dispersed throughout the neighbouring countries where they would settle to build their homes and synagogues.

169   Zerubbabel's Temple utterly destroyed by Antiochus Epiphanes, brother of the King of Syria.

AD

20–26   Herod the Great, the father of Herod Antipas (under whom Christ suffered), was a famous builder. He undertook the ambitious challenge of restoring the Temple to its former glory. The refurbished Second Temple was known as the Third Temple and it was finally destroyed by the Romans under Titus in AD70.

45–407   Roman Occupation of Britain.

800–1500	Free and Operative Societies of Architects, known as Freemasons, (not the rough artisans), emanating from the Collegia Artificium, came into existence as *Freemasons* in England, *Steinmetzen* in Germany, and the *Compagnonnage* in France. These Societies were secret and operative and they were engaged in erecting ecclesiastical and other buildings. Freemasonry as now practised is traced to this fraternity.
	Monks acted in the capacity of both Architect and Master to plan the buildings and supervise their erection. Thus non-operative as well as operative personnel became 'accepted'.
926	Annual Assembly of Operative Masons held at York under Prince Edwin, son of Athelstan. Old Lodge at York claims origin from this Assembly. See 1726.
1292	First known reference by English Masons to their workroom as 'Lodge'.
circa 1390	Regius Manuscript or Poem containing 'Antient Charges'. First known mention of the word *Freemason*.
circa 1410	Cooke Manuscript containing 'Antient Charges'.
1530	Statute of Edward III mentions the word *Freemason*.
1563	The word *Freemason* occurs in print for the first time in a book entitled *Dives Pragmaticus*.
1598	Earliest discovered record of Freemasonry in *Aichison Haven Scotch Lodge Minute Book*.
1646	Elias Ashmole made a Freemason in a Warrington Lodge. He writes in his diary that in the Gilds of (Operative) Stone and Freemasons the candidate had to be 'initiated' before he could learn his trade.
circa 1650	The Sloane Manuscript and Harleian manuscript contain references to 'Mason Word'.
1705	Records of Grand Lodge at York show that as early as this date it had a separate Constitution with a President and a Deputy President.
1714	Marks period of transition when Speculative Masons became so numerous and important that they overpowered the Operatives' Organisation.
1717	Grand Lodge convened. Anthony Sayer Grand Master. This Grand Lodge was later referred to as the 'Moderns'.
circa 1718	EA and FC Degrees included in one Degree, or the two separate

	Degrees worked in conjunction. These two Degrees embraced the whole of the elements of Craft Masonry.
1723	First Book of Constitutions (Moderns) published by Dr Anderson in which only two Degrees are mentioned — First, Apprentice part, Second FC or Master part. Charges amended, omitting direct reference to Christianity and a broader view taken of religious qualifications.
circa 1725	Third Degree acknowledged as an accepted rite, the subject matter being separated from the previous Degrees and the RA legends. Incorporation of the legend of d of Hiram Abif in the ritual. Committee of Charity established.
1726	Records of this date are found which show that the Old Lodge at York claims its origin from the Grand Assembly at York in AD926. Therefore of greater antiquity than the 1717 Grand Lodge of London, (the 'Moderns'). The Old Lodge at York proceeds to style itself the *Grand Lodge of all England*.
1738	Revised Edition of Book of Constitutions ('Moderns') published by Dr Anderson, in which the three degrees are recognised. First — Entered Apprentice, Second — Fellow Craft, Third — Master.
1744	The Royal Arch first worked as a separate Ceremony.
1751	*A Grand Lodge of England* according to the old institution formed. The members styled themselves as the 'York', 'Atholl' or 'Antients'. 'York' because they claimed that they had preserved the true traditions, like the masons of the old York Lodge, of the Operative Lodges and their Old Charges; 'Atholl' after their Grand Master, The Duke of Atholl; and 'Antients' because of their claim to greater antiquity than the 'Moderns'. Open war was declared by the 'Moderns' (original Grand Lodge of 1717) on the 'Antients'.
1755	Revised Edition of the Book of Constitutions ('Moderns') published.
1756	Laurence Dermott published the first Book of Laws or Constitutions of the 'Antients' under the title of 'Ahiman Rezon or a Help to a Brother'. (More correctly 'Voluntary Brethren').
1766	Revised edition of the Book of Constitutions ('Moderns').
1769	Earliest Record of Mark Masonry in a Speculative Body. Occurs in the opening Minutes of the Chapter of Friendship now No.

	257 Portsmouth. The Pro Grand Master Thomas Dunckerley was present. He made several of the Brethren Mark Masons. 'And each chuse their Mark'.
1776	Dedication of Freemasons' Hall, Great Queen Street, London.
1781	HRH Henry Frederick, Duke of Cumberland, elected Grand Master.
1789	'Moderns' develop the elaborate ritual of moral teaching based on the VSL and on their first Book of Constitutions.
1790	HRH George, Prince of Wales (afterwards King George IV) elected Grand Master.
1809	Basis of Agreement found by 'Moderns' and 'Antients'.
1813	HRH George the Prince Regent, (afterwards King George IV) resigns Grand Mastership and assumes title of Grand Patron. HRH the Duke of Sussex elected Grand Master. Joint Meeting of 'Moderns' and 'Antients'. HRH the Duke of Sussex, Grand Master, and HRH the Duke of Kent, Grand Master of the Atholl or Ancient Grand Lodge sign the Articles of Union on the 25th November.
1851	Bon-Accord Lodge of Mark Masters hold their first meeting in London.
1856	Formation of Grand Mark Lodge.
1857	Lord Leigh, First Grand Master of Grand Mark Lodge.

The Mark Benevolent Fund

Mark Masons are proud and happy to have their very own Fund of Benevolence, affectionately known as the Mark Benevolent Fund or MBF.

The Mark Benevolent Fund is a veritable part of the Mark Degree's remarkable history. In 1868 the then Grand Master, The Reverend Canon G R Portal became aware of the need of a Charity Fund which could move quickly to help a Brother or member of his family in distress. He believed that in a large number of instances the Charity could only be helpful and effective if it could surmount the time consuming formalities usually associated with petitions to Craft Charities. And so the Mark Benevolent Fund was born to give timely and advantageous help to those in need. Hence also came the origin of the MBF Motto, devised also by the Reverend Canon Portal. *Bis dat qui cito dat*, a Latin phrase meaning, *He gives twice who gives quickly.*

Today the Mark Benevolent Fund thrives on the generosity of Mark Master Masons governed by the Grand Lodge of Mark Master Masons of England and Wales and its Districts and Lodges Overseas. An all important source of funds for the Mark Benevolent Fund are the Charity Festivals, another idea by the Reverend Canon Portal which was catapulted into action in 1869 when the first MBF Charity Festival was held at the Mitre Hotel, Hampton Court. It raised the sum of £79.00 which at that time was considered a most satisfactory result.

The most recent Mark Benevolent Fund Festival held in the year 2001 by the Province of London raised the sum of £607,859.36.

A few Major Grants made from the Mark Benevolent Fund in the Year 2000 are as follows :

St John Ambulance Brigade	£2,000,000.00
Muscular Dystrophy	£10,000.00
AIA Autism Research	£25,000.00
Jubilee Masters Nurses Training	£2,500.00
The Flying Hospital	£24,155.00
St Andrews Hospice	£5,000.00
and many more.	

Since the establishment of the Mark Benevolent Fund in 1868, a total sum of £3,463,728.21 has been distributed in grants to petitioners, as calculated up to the 31st March, 2001.

Mark Masons have earned the right to be happy and proud of their Fund of Benevolence. But they are *not content.* They are ever anxious *to do even better.*

Operation Brotherly Love

The Province of London is undoubtedly the largest Province of Mark Master Masons in the world.

Operation Brotherly Love has been set up to meet the needs of distressed Brethren and their families within the Province of London who require urgent help, much in the same way as the Mark Benevolent Fund has been established to assist *all* Mark Masons and their dependants in distress in good time, with optimum benefit and relief.

Brotherly Love is supported financially by the London Lodges and it is expected that each Lodge will contribute one charity collection each year to the Fund. Such contributions are fortified and boosted with various fund raising activities. It is estimated that with a Fund of some £50,000 the Province will be able to deal with such claims as may be made on it. Care has been taken not to detract funds from the Mark Benevolent Fund which is the long term Mark Masons' Fund of Benevolence. We have emphasised already that we are 'The Friendly Degree' which has put a special emphasis on Brotherly Love and placed upon our Brother the highest possible valuation as a friend and companion.

Operation Brotherly Love is therefore not concerned with financial assistance alone. Lodges are being encouraged to appoint an Almoner or Care Officer who will be there for a Brother or his dependants when needed. Socrates used the strange term, *Enlightened Selfishness*, meaning that when we are thoughtful and do good to others, we are best to ourselves.

For a' that and a' that,
It's coming yet for a' that,
That man to man the world o'er
Shall brothers be for a' that.
Brother Robert Burns (1759–1796).

The Mark Masons' Anthem

Walk Beside Me

Chorus…
Don't walk in front of me, I may not follow,
Don't walk behind me, I may not lead,
Walk beside me, Walk beside me,
And be my friend, just be my friend.

Verse…
And we will bring the blind by a way they know not.
We will lead them in paths they have not known,
And we will turn the darkness to light before them
And the crooked things straight.

Chorus…
Don't walk in front of me, I may not follow,
Don't walk behind me, I may not lead,
Walk beside me, Walk beside me,
And be my friend, just be my friend.

Verse…
And we have pluck'd a few flow'rs,
Let us take them and plant them,
In every corner of our Province,
So they may spread their fragrance and their joy,
Where they are needed most.

Chorus…
Don't walk in front of me, I may not follow,
Don't walk behind me, I may not lead,
Walk beside me, Walk beside me,
And be my friend, just be my friend.

Extract from an old Persian poem translated as follows:

'Do not walk in front of me; I may not follow,
Do not walk behind me; I may not see you
Walk beside me I want you to be my friend'

By kind permission of RW Bro Roeinton B F Khambatta
Provincial Grand Master (London) 1991–1994

About the Author

WBro David Mitchell, PAGDC,
PPrGJW (London), PPrGrReg (Gloucestershire & Herefordshire), PRAMGR

David Mitchell was advanced into The King Solomon's Quarries Lodge No. 828 Jerusalem in 1967. He was Master of King Solomon's Quarries Lodge in 1979 and again in 1995.

A Past Master of Saint Ethelbert Lodge of Mark Masters No. 243 in the Province of Gloucestershire and Herefordshire, he was Founder Director of Ceremonies in Leofric Lodge of Mark Master Masons No. 1650.

He is also a Passé Maître (Past Master) of the French-speaking Lodge, Loge de Maître Maçons de Marque La France No. 459 where he held the office of Directeur des Cérémonies.

He has Provincial Grand Rank in Royal Ark Mariners. He is the Honorary Secretary of the Quatuor Coronati Correspondence Circle for the Province of Herefordshire. A Fellow of the British Institute of Management and Member of the Chartered Institute of Marketing, he spent his professional working life in London. He is now retired and living in Hereford.

Final Word

The Author, WBro David Mitchell, shortly after his Advancement into Mark Masonry remarked to his Sponsor, a well-known Grand Officer, Dr G L C Colenso-Jones, that Craft Masonry without the Mark Ceremony seemed rather like a bird without its feathers.

Dr G L C Colenso-Jones, who was later to become the Rt WBro Pro Grand Master, with a twinkle in his eye, replied, 'I'm sure you are right, David, and one day many others will think the same.'

Index

92